Date Due

2 Jan '51			
18 Jan '51			
10 Feb '51			
18 Sep '51			

THE PURSUIT OF PLENTY

The PURSUIT

of PLENTY

The Story of Man's Expanding Domain

By A. G. MEZERIK

Author of *The Revolt of the South and West*

Years of the modern! years of the unperform'd!
Your horizon rises, I see it parting away for
more august dramas,
I see not America only, not only Liberty's nation
but other nations preparing,
I see tremendous entrances and exits, new
combinations, the solidarity of races ...
WALT WHITMAN

HARPER & BROTHERS NEW YORK

THE PURSUIT OF PLENTY

FIRST EDITION

H-Z

To all those people throughout the world
who face the future with confidence because they are doing something about it

CONTENTS

PREFACE ix

ACKNOWLEDGMENTS xi

I. IRRESISTIBLE VS. IMMOVABLE 1

II. ENDS AND MEANS 5

III. DESTROYER OR CREATOR 14

IV. LEADERS OF THE REAR GUARD 19

V. POLITICAL OIL ON THE FIRE 34

VI. SHORTAGE AT THE GRASS ROOTS 45

VII. CUSTOMS AND TABOOS—AMERICAN STYLE 55

VIII. NATURE IN A STRAITJACKET 63

IX. MOUNTAINTOP TO RIVER BOTTOM 80

X. MEN AND NATURE 97

XI. POLITICAL BRIDGEHEADS 110

XII. A DROP TO DRINK 122

XIII. LONG STEPS TO A GREAT GOAL 135

XIV. EARTH CONTROL AND BIRTH CONTROL 147

XV. UNIVERSAL RESOURCES 162

XVI. THE NEW GEOLOGIC FORCE 176

XVII. MIND OVER MATTER 184

XVIII. CREATIVE TOMORROWS 192

INDEX 205

PREFACE

The reasons for this book are to be found in the vital statistics of the world. In many parts of the world population is increasing rapidly. The problems of providing future supplies of food and other essential resources in amounts sufficient to assure new millions a fair standard of living present a challenge—by comparison with which the usual headaches presented in the morning papers are puny. I believe, on the basis of the evidence, that we can meet the challenge.

The pessimists who are now so popular take the opposite view. They believe that we are doomed—we have only a few years to live. They view the world as a sinking ship on which all activity is ridiculous unless it is confined to immediate practical measures. The picture of the inevitable end which they have conjured up is probably just as real to them as was the vision of those many fanatics who, over the ages, have seen the certainty of a divinely inspired conflagration which on a certain scheduled day would consume the earth and all on it. And when people were less informed about the workings of nature than now, millions were terrified and paralyzed by the dire prophecies of these seers.

Today the modern seers have similarly terrified num-

bers of people, this time not with predictions of a divinely
instigated catastrophe but of one instigated by Man himself. The result is that any attempt to visualize—on the
basis of evidence—an opposite pattern of the flowering of
society is derided as "wonderful-world-of-the-future"
imaginings, perhaps suitable for Sunday supplements, but
certainly not for serious consideration. In the framework
of the thinking of the pessimists no research is worth while
because research takes years and they give us only minutes.

Were we all to be persuaded by this pessimistic inevitability we would be indeed paralyzed, for to admit the
possibility that society will not exist fifty years from now
cancels all point in any activity with an aim of more than
immediate usefulness. But the predictions of the pessimists
are cut of the same cloth as were those of the earlier prophets of doom. They can mean as little. The evidence indicates that even as Man has the power to destroy, he has
the power to create, and that ability for constructive action
grows as minds develop and tools improve—so that do
we decide to will it, we can live in a peaceful world of
abundance.

A. G. M.

New York City
June, 1950

ACKNOWLEDGMENTS

The Public Affairs Institute, which has demonstrated in many ways its great interest in the better utilization and expansion of natural resources, has sponsored this volume jointly with the National Farmers Union and the Brotherhood of Railroad Trainmen. Dewey Anderson, Executive Director of the Public Affairs Institute, and James G. Patton, President of the National Farmers Union, were particularly unflagging in their support and help from the beginning. Others in these organizations gave me generously of their time and knowledge, as did many scientists, government administrators, and specialists on whom I have called for help and information. Many of the chapters dealing with the Missouri Valley have their source in discussions at the Missouri Valley Conference that took place in Washington.

The continuing consultation with Morris L. Cooke has a special place. His unstinting help and wise counsel were of inestimable value. Marie Mezerik has contributed notably both as to the subject matter and as to the making of the book.

All the interpretations of this wealth of material, so generously given me, are, of course, my own and the judgment as to their validity is in the reader's hands.

A. G. M.

THE PURSUIT OF PLENTY

CHAPTER I

Irresistible vs. Immovable

THE commentators, the pundits, and the politicians agree on one thing. We are ending the toughest, roughest half-century in the memory of Man. Not just a hard winter or a long drought but an era of famine and tyranny, of round after round of wars and revolutions in which the art of war advanced fantastically and destruction became incredibly easy.

Even in their peaceful endeavors, people had shown a power to destroy their environment, to demolish the very resources on which they depend for food and clothing and shelter. Neglect, complacency, ignorance, and greed were transforming large areas into semi-deserts. Unpinned from the earth by overcropping and other bad agricultural practices, the soil swirled away in dust storms or was washed into rivers. Unbridled industries polluted streams; sewage poisoned drinking supplies. Proud cities faced a thirsty future, as surface sources dried up and underground water sank deeper and deeper into the recesses of the earth.

This was the time and the hour for pumping—not only

water but oil and gas. It was the time for ripping out the ores from the bowels of the earth. It seemed that men were possessed of the notion that nothing usable or useful to Man, beast, or nature should remain. It was a time for cutting—as stumps in shrinking forests mutely testified; the sounds of birds singing and the rustle of wildlife in the brush diminished with each disappearing tree.

It was a curious half-century. The four horsemen rode as never before, but more people were alive than ever before. Neither war, nor disease nor famine had curtailed the growth of the population. The seeds of time were diverse and burgeoned on many fronts. Though war could not be curbed, disease did feel the controlling impress of Man's hand. As the ability to destroy was shod with seven-league boots so, too, was the ability to prolong life and to make it easier. It became possible for every man to enjoy luxuries which the greatest potentate in all the centuries which had gone before could not command, despite his millions of slaves and his wealth.

Almost total paradoxes were everywhere. As gardens were turned into deserts and cities into rubble, so other deserts were turned back into gardens and cities almost miraculously appeared in new or ancient areas. As soils were eroded, so the earth's strength was restored. As waters were poisoned, so they were cleansed. As destruction marched through many forests, so some were planted. As the sources of food were exhausted, new potential horns of plenty made their appearance. As the guts of the earth were violently torn out, substitutes for minerals and fuels came into being. War, irresponsibility, and overuse had reduced huge regions to barren waste, but a TVA had revitalized a whole area, and in Scandinavia, Russia, and many another country other areas had been brought into balance with nature.

For fifty years a struggle has raged between mounting forces of destruction and of construction. The conflict has left its scars everywhere and on everyone. Displaced persons by the million, disconsolately—and all too often fruitlessly—roaming the earth in search of a home and a haven, all but wash out remembrance that in this half century the exploration, the mapping, and the colonizing of the entire planet have been completed. Military expeditionary forces, pouring organized brutality into peoples and cities, blur the fact that the North and the South Poles have been penetrated by armies of peace, that the fastnesses of the deepest jungles have opened their secrets to men without guns. The antiaircraft beams and the flare of bomb-set fires dim the meaning of the achievement of harnessing electricity on a wide scale, of lighting homes and easing the burdens of countless millions who had lived in darkness and squalor since time without memory. The fear of atomic death all but blots out the vitalization of knowledge which is implicit in wresting from nature one of its greatest secrets, atomic fission.

These are physical manifestations of a half century. The paradoxes dominate ideas even more. Hitler and his crop of tyrants have shaken faith and belief in freedom. Gas chambers, concentration camps and police control over thought and action have almost erased from our minds the truth that these eerie fifty years have also marked an immense advance in human welfare, justice, and liberty in both hemispheres. Higher standards of living, of health, and welfare have come to huge areas of the globe as have ideas of democracy, justice, and liberty.

In all this, it might well seem that the irresistible forces of construction have met the immovable forces of destruction, with frustration the result. But men are behind these two forces and men can make a decision as to which will win. Both forces—constructive and destructive—are great and dynamic, pushed and promoted by single-minded men living under ideas of their making and driven by desires. Over each group of men hangs one overwhelming power, science. The leverage and the strength by which both forces have come so far is in the works of science.

As the curtain rises on the second half of this climactic century, the dominant question is—what will men do with the great and vastly accelerating power of science? It is for men to decide whether we will make an overpowering majority out of these human beings who seek to follow the line of constructive achievement which runs so clear through the first fifty years—or if by complacence, neglect, or ignorance we will permit supreme power, including that of science, to remain in the grip of those who have painted a bloody ribbon across the half century.

CHAPTER II

Ends and Means

THE basic difference between the new and the old, between the constructive and the destructive, is not to be found alone in attitudes about who owns what—or in the conventional terms which describe forms of political and economic organization. Capitalism and communism reveal little of the essence. It is in the attitude of men toward their natural resources, base of the pyramid on which society rests, that one great part of the reality can be found. The other essential is in how men regard men, what importance they attach to human dignity and the flowering of the individual. Nowhere does the essential difference, and the conflict between old and new, come up more clearly than in the attitudes and actions which grow out of the realization that the numbers of people on earth are increasing and that resources are being more rapidly consumed.

Because of science and public health people live longer. More are now alive than at any time in history. Each wants to stay alive, to eat well, to have a good home. It is clear that this can only happen if food is supplied in ever increasing amounts—if spiralling amounts of wood, minerals, and other necessities can be provided. Otherwise the vast majority of the 2¼ billions on earth now and the millions who will be added in the next half century are doomed to starvation and poverty.

This is the central question of our time. The old-fashioned man answers it by making a formal bow in the direction of the necessity for conserving natural resources and then—without further ado or investigation—puts his finger on Man himself as the great menace. Fearing the oncoming of too many people, the old-fashioned men seek arbitrarily to hold down the numbers of human beings in the world and thereby maintain their own privileges, wealth, and power.

The old-fashioned men maintain that most of the mistakes which the world has made with regard to nature and resources are in the direction of having permitted Man to live longer. However that is the second mistake in the order of importance. The first is to let most children get born. To further this notion and to give this conception some basis in history, they have revived the Malthusian Law. The followers of Malthus are now many. Once again the gloomy doctor's *Essay on Population*, which in the nineteenth century had such grim consequences for the poor of England, has been dusted off and propounded. Malthus declared that the tendency of population is to press increasingly heavily upon subsistence. Population,

operating without the benefit of various natural and im-
posed checks, tends to increase in geometric proportion
while food supplies increase only in arithmetical proportion.

To avert the inevitable starvation which he foresaw
for all, Malthus wanted the poor to practice birth control
and if they didn't do it voluntarily, he had other more
stringent methods in mind. One was to starve whole families. Malthus put it this way:

It appears to me that we are bound in justice and honour
formally to disclaim the *right* of the poor to support. To this
end, I should propose a regulation to be made, declaring that
no child born from any marriage, taking place after the expira-
tion of a year from the date of the law, and no illegitimate child
born two years from the same date, should ever be entitled to
parish assistance. . . . If any man choose to marry without a
prospect of being able to support a family . . . all parish assistance should be denied him; he should be left to the uncertain
support of private charity. He should be taught to know, that
the laws of nature, which are the laws of God, had doomed him
and his family to suffer for disobeying their oft-repeated ad-
monitions; that he had no claim of *right* on society for the
smallest portion of food, beyond that which his labour would
fairly purchase.

Remember that one part of Dr. Malthus' theory had to
do with food. But where increased supplies of food were
promised, he liked those ideas not at all, since he feared
that better eating would increase population and only
bring more evil. On this basis Malthus opposed a scheme

to provide every laborer having three children with a half acre of land and grass for one or two cows. He similarly put thumbs down on a proposal made by Cobbett to give every married laborer an acre of waste land. Obviously, Malthus was less concerned with plans by which more subsistence could be gained than he was with fear of people— poor people. In 1834, the rich—operating now by right of the "natural law" propounded by Malthus—abolished outdoor relief for the able-bodied poor. Thus the upper classes took some cash benefits immediately. The rich also took spiritual solace from Dr. Malthus. They had been given a comfortable and comforting theory. The Malthus theory was like an umbrella snugly protecting the good consciences of the rich from responsibility for the rain of vice, misery, starvation, and disease which poured down on their fellowmen. Since poverty was obviously ordained and inevitable, the consequences of it were but a purge employed by nature to eliminate the unfit. It was all part of a continuous, though unfortunately painful, spur toward human progress. Under this theory, to provide food would be to fly in the face of nature since, once fed, more children would begotten. The poor therefore must remain condemned to eternal misery. The rich, having found in Dr. Malthus what they were looking for to give them serenity and save them money, reacted notably—confining their giving to a few crumbs of charity and to promoting a brand of religion which would spend most of its time helping the poor rise above the sufferings of their daily life.

It all sounds grim, and the kind of thing that in a history book shows up by contrast the great advances to which we, in our time, have attained. But change the name from Malthus to William Vogt and the story becomes as contemporary as today. These ideas of Malthus are the very ones which are today applauded, espoused, and propagandized by a whole group of neo-Malthusians.

Much of the time this attitude—expressed in so many actions and in currently popular books—is wrapped in the plausible cloak of conservation, to which obeisance is always made. The neo-Malthusians start with a profoundly true observation. Man has done damage to nature. By his abuse of the land and the water resources he is depriving himself of his ability to sustain a large population. Then they leap across a wide terrain of fact to make their main point—the deterioration of nature's resources is now so well advanced that doom is just around the corner, unless population growth is curbed drastically.

They contend that this desperate situation is world-wide and that the poisonous overpopulation exists to an aggravated degree everywhere. Theirs is always the old story of the fear that living organisms may multiply too fast. Everyone has, at one time or another, been regaled with figures which prove irrefutably that, on the basis of their rate of multiplication, any number of creatures could soon cover the earth's surface. I read only the other day that for certain bacteria the speed of their reproduction—as it could theoretically colonize the earth—approaches the velocity of sound. As children, all of us did some simple arithmetic which started with a pair of rabbits. Obviously theoretically possible birth and death rates are different from reality, else we would right now be elbowing rabbits in order to walk down Fifth Avenue. The new twist on these older versions is to ignore the rabbits and concentrate on Mankind. The old-fashioned men find cause for alarm everywhere. For our own country they recommend an optimum population—if the United States is to maintain a continuing high standard of living—of 100 million people, a figure popular with all those who fear Man as the greatest danger.

Fear is, however, not the best motivation for seeking objective truth, however much it may serve to arouse emotions. It does not tell us much about the true facts of population growth and cycles, both a matter of scientific inquiry. One might suppose that, since an interpretation of the facts about population growth is the essence of the theory on which so many of the old-fashioned men predicate their attitudes to human beings, they would use a scientific method to lay out those facts. However, with great nonchalance almost all ignore the findings of all population experts who cannot be constricted into their Procrustean bed. An important body of evidence on population trends exists. Some experts figure the maximum population of the United States—barring immigration or other importation—at no more than 200 millions, surely not a catastrophic figure in a land that is as big and as rich as ours.

Raymond Pearl, recognized as an outstanding expert on population, estimated, on the basis of his study of the population figures between 1660 and 1932, that the limit of the current cycle of growth for the world population is two billion six hundred and forty-five million and that it "will be closely approached around A.D. 2100, provided nothing happens in the meantime to alter seriously the present trends of productivity." The world population today is 2¼ billion. This means that the expected addition to the world population is less than one-half billion people. While this is a large increase it is spread over the next 150 years. However, were the increase in population much larger—as some believe—it will not necessarily bring hunger in its wake. Colin Clark, Australian population expert and economist, sums up the entire problem of whether population growth is outrunning the capacity to provide food with the calculation that the world's population is increasing by one per cent each year while ability to provide food is growing at the rate of 1½%. "The problem," he says, "is soluble, if we go about it the right way."

With all this talk about so many people now alive, the casual reader might surmise that men everywhere have been forced by overcrowding to live cheek by jowl, with only an occasional mountain or ocean to relieve the congestion. The picture painted by the economist, L. Brentano, is different. His computation showed that if a square meter were assigned to each living man, and if all men were placed close to one another, they would not fully occupy the small area of Lake Constance between the borders of Switzerland and Bavaria. Since this lake is only 207 square miles in area, or about the same size as the city of Chicago and less than half of that of Los Angeles, the mass of men on the earth seems far from having created an intolerable congestion.

These calculations and forecasts have no part in the dogma of the old-fashioned men. Nor do these men deal in the techniques of science and education—including birth control—which the modern man sees as imperative toward stabilizing populations at high standards of living. They have thought for so long of men in terms of markets when they can afford to buy, or—if not—as a source of cheap labor that they find it impossible to view Man as a re-source, the one unit of living matter capable of expanding, even creating, the other resources.

Yet to the modern man, the most significant of all developments of the turbulent decades through which we have lived is the recognition that Man is himself a re-source, as valuable as the rivers and the fields—and ever so much more desirable than the gold and the diamonds which Man still treasures above all things which he takes from nature's storehouse. The premise of those who see hope and promise in the future is simple. Man is the back-ground resource. It is he who finds the uses and the values which are inherent in all the other resources. More than that, Man creates new resources which never before ex-isted—and since he has opened the fields of science and technology, he does this increasingly. This quality of innovation has made Man more valuable to nature's whole system of interrelationships.

This guiding idea and motivation runs side by side with the knowledge that human intelligence is now a major ingredient in natural resources and it increases the effectiveness of all others—animal, vegetable, and mineral. The human mind is an alchemist, turning the dross of common things into the gold of the resources we want and need. The old is perfected. More food comes from a single plant, more yield from the acre. We create new things, we open up titanic forces of energy.

As a result of all this, modern men see a startling new pattern in human activities, a new relationship with nature. They add up the constructive achievements of a half century to a sum of capacities and tools which no form of life ever had before. Inside this new relationship, population and resources can complement each other. Once Man is viewed as the greatest resource, it quickly emerges that his increased well-being is the major purpose of conserving and utilizing other natural resources. The end for the modern man is the assurance of the highest possible level of physical, mental, and social well-being for all. His conviction is that, given wise decisions, proper organization and direction, human well-being is not only an end but the only means by which the natural resources of the world are most likely to be conserved and developed. That—and not how to get rid of Man—is obviously the problem.

CHAPTER III

Destroyer or Creator

The sword sang on the barren heath,
    The sickle in the fruitful field:
The sword he sang a song of death,
But could not make the sickle yield.
—WILLIAM BLAKE

THOUGH the apostles of yesterday fear men, they are proud of their long view of Man's history. Committed to the power and universality of destruction, they examine the history of mankind and find that it is Man who is responsible for practically all the deserts, for all the eroded land, for all the barrens. They range throughout all history—from Man's emergence to the present—to make their point, contending that all previous civilizations fell because Man mistreated the land. Their conclusion is that our own civilization is on the threshold of the same downfall.

But it is far from a settled and proved historical fact that Man's treatment of the land was the cause of the disappearance of previous civilizations. No less an authority than America's leading soil expert, Charles E. Kellogg, Chief of the Division of Soil Survey, United States Department of Agriculture, believes that soil deterioration was not the agent of decline but a result. He thinks the deterioration of the soil was the effect of deeper causes and he says, "Generally, when a rural population becomes poverty stricken, it fails to maintain its soil. An exploited people pass on their suffering to the land. Low prices, disease and wars are all important causes. Things get on a hand-to-mouth or year-to-year basis. . . . Where farmers can take a long view of production, there are very few instances of conflict between those practices that give most return and those that maintain the soil. . . ." Low prices and exploitation are root causes. Proof that this is so is close at hand in our own Tennessee Valley.

TVA came into being during the great depression when Americans were receptive to daring innovations and the grip of the old-fashioned men had relaxed momentarily. It was conceived, and it has been carried out as a practical measure, to save a region which in 150 years of uncontrolled competition was devastated as though by war. The century and a half of destruction in the Tennessee Valley was part of the cost of building the most highly industrialized country in the world. Industrialization is indeed desirable, but the Tennessee Valley is irrefutable proof that—in our own country—it was achieved in spite of ignorance. Tragic waste and appalling expense—much of which was unnecessary, marked the growth of our industrial might. The men who place the private right to do public damage at the head of their lists of freedoms had pillaged the Tennessee Valley. As part of their basic philosophy, they fought the efforts of scientists of all kinds, of advanced thinkers and of such forward-looking statesmen as Senator George Norris, who for years tried to create the Tennessee Valley Authority. Today they still fight, though in TVA intelligent planning and good administration have been tied together into a whole which has been voted an outstanding beacon in a world where sound management of land and water has been the great exception. Not only Americans but citizens from every land travel through the Tennessee Valley, inspecting its works and its results. Americans, having seen the Valley, return to their own regions, many times determined to extend the principle of TVA operation into the river valleys where they live. Foreigners return to their native lands, often taking alumni of the TVA with them, and begin to plan to harness their waterfalls, control their floods, and increase the yield of the land and the standard of living of their people.

In the books written and the speeches made by those who hold that Man is solely a destroyer, conservation is always applauded. But in action, they never applaud TVA. Yet, if the purpose of conservation is, as accepted by most people, to provide a better floor for the life of Man—then TVA has demonstrated great benefits.

The face of the land has been changed. The ways of earning a living have been made easier. A great new regional center of industry has emerged. Farming is being liberated from the slavery of trying to get a crop from worn-out soil. The newly created supply of electric power has made possible a huge production of fertilizer, even as it has liberated farmers from back-breaking toil. The lives of farmers grow easier. Health is improved for all. Better living has vitalized education, libraries, and other phases of community life. Since TVA came into being in 1934, acreage yields have gone up in the Tennessee Valley as much as 50 per cent; corn, a harmful row crop, has decreased about 20 per cent in acreage. Tenancy has declined by 38.1 per cent; 200 million TVA-produced trees have been planted in 136 thousand acres of eroded and otherwise unproductive land. This begins to add up to a conclusion opposite to the thesis of the old-fashioned men— one that would prove that the potential of the earth is great enough, if determined action is taken, to support the population now on it, as well as of those who might be born in the half century ahead.

The conclusion becomes clearer when TVA benefits are evaluated from the statistics which reveal the rise in the standard of living of the people in the Valley. Industrialization, for instance, has increased wages and salaries drawn from manufacturing from 1933's $81,300,000 to 1946's $496,800,000. During the same period, annual per capita income has increased from $148 to $758.

In the Tennessee Valley not only are resources conserved, even expanded, but the population has risen 20 per cent—or more than 400,000. The standard of living has gone up for each member of that population, new as well as old. All these deductions and observations about TVA are well known. They have not, for one moment, persuaded those who talk so loudly about hopeless futures to drop their violent opposition to TVA or to any of the many projects which it has sparked.

The old-fashioned man, be he a neo-Malthusian or an industrial giant, sees only the old-fashioned damage. That this damage still continues is—and should be—pointed out. But the story is incomplete and misleading unless it is equally emphasized that on the same planet where damage is still being done Man is creating ever widening areas of reclamation, greater regions of conservation, and new synthetic foods and resources. As significant as abuse of the land is Man's successful effort to find new usability of plant forms formerly ignored, to open new vistas of agriculture and tree and fish farming, and to experiment with the possibilities of the Arctic and the tropics, both unsuited hitherto for human habitation, but conceivable sources for food. However, to paint in these realities and hopeful prospects—as true as are the dire predictions of immediate doom—takes optimists, men who believe that the very young race of *Homo sapiens* is only just emerging from infancy into maturity, instead of forthwith heading over the precipice of extinction. It takes another attribute. The ability to see and the desire to use—in the public interest— the great new resources, science and industry.

CHAPTER IV

Leaders of the Rear Guard

W HEN the leaders of the rear guard talk, they pay great lip service to the benefits of science in raising the standard of living. When they act, it is many times to constrict science so that it will not be used in creating a new interrelationship between Man and nature.

They put their greatest emphasis always on the danger which is so implicit in the fact that science has made it easier for Man to destroy himself. That Man, instead of destroying himself and his environment, can improve both, and use science and the products of industry with which to do it, cannot fit into their thinking because it runs counter to their interests and their ideas. This is not only true of the neo-Malthusian writers but of those "men of action", who disregard the public interest in favor of their private profit.

Their unremitting fight against TVA, first of the great modern projects in the public interest, is especially revealing. It is not alone an action against the Tennessee Valley but against the integrated development of the Missouri

Valley, of the Jordan River Valley in Palestine, of the San Francisco in Brazil—of the attempt everywhere to lift the public interest above private gain and to use science for the expansion and conservation of resources. Against these projects, vested interests—corporate, government, and individual—present a united front which is ceaselessly busy.

In our own country the "men of action" who are the leaders in this remorseless fight are the bankers for and operators of the privately owned power companies, which in TVA were the first to feel the impact of new methods carried out in the interests of all the people. The utility company methods have been complex, aggressive, tireless, and devious. The electrical industry has invaded the political field through its National Association of Electric Companies, headed by a $65,000 per year executive. Through this organization, the power companies have concentrated on political obstruction designed to stop TVA and the extension of regional developments everywhere. They were, and are, particularly venomous toward the creation of a Missouri Valley Authority, the very project dictated by necessity, logic, and evolution as next on the American list for regional reconstruction. The utility technique is simple, though paradoxical—condemning proponents of TVA as political while they themselves politick every step of the way.

Using their political methods, the utility companies have succeeded in removing officials who serve in the public interest rather than their own. In October, 1949, they led a successful attempt to deny Congressional approval to President Truman's renomination of Leland Olds as Federal Power Commissioner. Olds had popular support. Along with many prominent individuals, representatives of The American Public Power Association, National Rural Electric Cooperative Association, and many other organizations testified that Olds—strong advocate of TVA—had effectively and fairly regulated the utility industries in the public interest during his ten years on the Commission.

But that was the difficulty. The electric utilities, of course, did not say so; instead they confined themselves to the smear of "communism," digging out Olds's writings of twenty years ago as proof. Despite much more recent and more powerful proof that Olds's actions had saved millions of dollars for the public and despite wide grassroots support, the old-fashioned men jettisoned Olds. Less than a month later, the FPC, minus Leland Olds, handed the great Pacific Gas & Electric Company of California a fifty-year license to build and operate hydroelectric plants in the Kings River development. This was a body blow to public power and the plans for integrated development of the Great Central Valley Project in California. To smoke screen this type of political barrage, which goes on continuously, the public relations departments of the industry have hoisted their old "free enterprise" flag and, in a flood of slick paid propaganda (1949 budget $1,000,000) in big magazines, on the air, and in newspapers—tiny country weeklies as well as huge metropolitan dailies—have attempted to bury the memory of Insull and Hopson, of the water in their stocks, the franchises in their socks, and the many skeletons in their closets—but most of all to kill off the TVA type of development.

Though their activities take them into national promotional programs, the utility chiefs do not for a moment neglect local propaganda. In every town and hamlet where private utilities have influence the private power chiefs arrange speakers for luncheon meetings, buy local advertising, and spread the word against "communism" in the TVA. All through the Missouri Valley the local henchmen of the utility chiefs work feverishly in and out of the State legislatures to stymie the growth of regional support for the creation of an authority in that region. In the far Northwest the private power interests fight the Colombia Valley Authority with the same relentlessness which they show against TVA. They fight it even while they admit, as they did recently in the State of Washington, that only the national government can or will make the necessary investment to provide the additional power now so badly needed. All this far-flung activity requires a huge network, a good part of which is not visible to the naked eye.

Aboveground is the Edison Electric Institute, the trade associations, and the utility lobby which spends increasing amounts of money each year, their 1949 budget, $330,000. Underground are certain State Public Service Commis-

sions, and some individual commissioners; some city officials, city legislatures; certain "impartial" newspapers, tax
associations; "small businessmen's organizations," educators and Congressmen; and most important, a few inside
semisocial cliques—command units where over-all policies
are determined, subject only to the supreme dictum of the
top banking circles.

The ultimate goal is, of course, to stop the government
from producing power, not only where they now do it—
as at TVA and Bonneville—but in any future development
such as the Missouri Valley. This is a difficult objective to
attain in the face of the fact that increasingly large numbers of human beings on farms, in homes, and in shops are
prepared to fight to the death for continued government
ownership and operation of the power-producing facilities.
Therefore the utility interests have more limited objectives in relation to their big target.

Since the establishment of TVA the government agencies have held the right, granted them by Congress, to
wholesale the power generated at the public dams. In
pursuance of this right the agencies have given priorities
for the purchase of their power to municipalities and Rural
Electrical operative units. Though the power chiefs have
always made the lion's share of their profits from distribution and not from wholesaling, they have pulled out all
the stops on the free enterprise organ to lament the unfair
competition which this action represents. And the power
chiefs have been partially successful in winning this limited

objective since in California the output of the great Shasta
Dam goes almost exclusively to the colossal Pacific Gas &
Electric rather than to the many growing cities.

Objective number two is double barrelled, designed to
stop existing government power-producing agencies from
expanding, and at the same time to keep them from using
their present equipment with a maximum of efficiency.
TVA has operated and owned, since its inception, several
steam plants, the output of which is essential to stabilizing
the power which they produce from falling water. TVA
needed another such plant. The power lobby made an intensive fight against this projected plant and the in-fight-
ing revealed some very interesting attitudes. They fought
this plant despite the fact that the area to be served had
no privately owned utilities able to take over the load. The
power chiefs, despite their well-advertised allegiance to the
American Standard of Living, were willing to see a ceiling
put on that standard—for those of their fellow Americans
who happen to live in areas exclusively served by publicly owned power facilities. They carried the day. The
steam plant was denied by the 80th Congress.

But TVA is, by its very existence, creating the strength
among the people of the Valley to fight for TVA's future,
against the enemies of tomorrow. The 138 municipally
owned power companies and farmers' electrical cooperatives have been tempered in previous assaults upon the
TVA. The newspapers and the Chambers of Commerce

of the towns which have benefited from the Valley's development support TVA on its record—and the growing trade union movement is taking up its share of the load. Through years of vigilance, TVA's own administrative leadership has evolved—among its most important achievements—techniques with which to defend its accomplishments. This coalition is strong and it never stopped fighting for the steam plant. It was their insistence which finally turned the tide. The 81st Congress reversed its predecessor.

The people of other regions have not yet been welded into such strong fighting groups. They still wait for action. Another steam plant was denied by the 81st Congress for the Great Central Valley Project of California, where it is absolutely essential to the economic operation of the ambitious irrigation project already under way. The power chiefs publicly applaud all who speak of the necessity for more food to provide for America's growing population. Yet in action they have held down this attempt to create greater food production in California's Central Valley. They do it wherever public power is involved. In the Oklahoma-Arkansas region, the flow of the rivers is so irregular that no amount of hydro power can be used economically without additional steam plants. Nevertheless the power industry has succeeded in stopping this essential project.

Another way in which these men deny to the public the benefit of utilizing their own resources is to slow down such new public developments as they cannot hope to stop entirely. They put their money and their support behind a horse which won't run very far or very fast. This is the technique along the St. Lawrence River and in the Missouri Valley, as it was previously along the Columbia where the power chiefs, once they saw that they could not further hold up the development, got behind the Army Engineers—on the record an excellent way of slowing to a walk any large-scale development. And there are other limited objectives, some of which are, at this writing, almost in the hands of the power chiefs.

They hope to take the electricity, generated by public power, from the dams and then—distributing it over their own lines—derive from its sale at high prices the huge profits for which their mouths have been watering these many years. For the moment they will settle for a little less—they will take the electricity from the end of the government-built transmission line—anywhere as long as they get it. Meanwhile they have enlisted their henchmen in the Chamber of Commerce of the United States in a crusade to get TVA to charge more for government-produced electricity, a device by which they hope to avoid decreasing their own sometimes exorbitant rates.

An important corollary of all this activity is that this country, with its expanding population and its greater industrial needs, is not getting electric power at prices low enough to be used in amounts sufficient to enable widescale development of resources. The role which electricity plays as the integrator of resource conservation is clear in regional developments such as TVA and the proposed Missouri Valley Authority, both of which are so vigorously opposed by the utility chiefs.

Approach the problem of a river basin from any single standpoint—flood control, navigation, or power—and full control and rounded development seem remote. Approach it from the point of view of a single locality and its needs, and the solution appears impracticable and costly. Put all these resources together on a valley-wide and multiple-purpose basis and the goal of maximum and best use is within reach. The key which unlocks every resource is electricity. It is the common denominator of all, the open sesame for rounded development.

Electric power is a natural basis for region-wide planning. It places emphasis on valley-wide coordination, which is essential if the development is to progress. More, it helps pay the way for all the work, since it provides a true economic justification for water storage, which in turn is an essential part of any comprehensive river basin program designed to provide—in addition to power—flood control, pollution abatement, domestic water supply, irrigation, navigation, and recreation.

Electric power is the prime force in creating diversification of agriculture. It brings more profitable farm operation. In industry it makes possible a basis for diversification. Finally, electric power, when developed from falling water, is important in the conservation of the country's exhaustible energy resources, particularly oil and natural gas.

Electric power also means conservation of labor. What

a man can produce is almost directly proportional to the number of kilowatt-hours of electricity at his disposal. Electricity saves human energy even as it conserves the individual by providing him with a better working environment.

The electric motor has transformed the conditions in which Man works. Factories, once dark, unsanitary, and noisy—with overhead shafting and dangerous belting—have been converted into modern buildings powered by separate motors. In the first forty years of this century, electrification of factory machines has grown from almost nothing to approximately 85 per cent. During this time, while employment in manufacturing almost doubled, the total machine load increased nearly six times.

In that forty-year span, with hours of labor decreasing, the output of each worker doubled. Physical production quadrupled from 1900 to 1940. The value of the products manufactured increased at an even faster pace.

This is conservation, and it is more than conservation. It creates more than before—which is a distinguishing mark of the modern trend. The rule holds when applied to human labor and it holds equally when applied to the conservation of present resources and the use of raw materials which, without electricity, would otherwise hardly have been usable. In the forefront of this constructive development are the newer metallurgical and chemical industries, aluminum, steel, chlorine, ferro-alloys, and magnesium which already use one-third of all the electrical energy consumed by industry. These industries have made clay and minerals from the oceans usable—bringing new resources into being.

In conserving more familiar ores, electricity has made possible an almost unlimited number of methods for extracting metals from ores. In fact, conservation of low-grade manganese and of low-grade iron ores cannot be achieved without electricity.

This is the tiniest glimpse at the part which ample supplies of electric power play in furthering conservation through industrial processes. It does an equally important conservation job on the farm. Labor saving, elimination of spoilage, utilization of waste, processing of products for market, and increasing of the farms' self-sufficiency—all these are essential for stable prosperity and all are made possible by rural use of electricity, so long opposed by the private utility companies. The farmer who has the benefit of electricity can go forward with scientific steps looking to conservation of the soil.

Electricity forms a tie already binding industrial and agricultural research. Important strides in finding new uses for agricultural products are providing a sound basis for establishing new rural industries. In this field—at once conservation and expansion—developments are numerous. Given widely distributed power supply, they offer tremendous possibilities in the way of restoring balanced rural economies. In itself that creation would constitute a major achievement in conservation.

Freedom from back-breaking labor, conservation of old resources, and creation of new resources are made possible by electricity. Its cumulative social value is great and nowhere more than in its power to do away, finally and forever, with colonial regions, especially inside our own country. The wholly undemocratic state of economic bondage in which our South and West is kept can be changed. With regional development based on electric power it is possible to interweave agriculture with industry. In the West this would mean the reopening of the vast intermountain frontier which was by-passed in the great rush of eighty years ago when the railroads were joined into a transcontinental line. Today the colonizer will be the integrated development of the resources of the Missouri River and particularly the cheap electric power with which to work them.

Cheap electric power will bring better results for the West than did the coming of the railroads. The railroads were built—and are still owned—by the old-fashioned men. Their idea was, and is, to make the West into a colonial empire and to carry away the West's raw resources. Cheap power is, on the contrary, only obtainable through public development and ownership. With the cramping hand and mind of the old-fashioned men removed, the West could build a balanced development and a prosperity based upon a diversified economy—never permitted them in all the days of the rule of the old robber barons.

Electricity changes the economic factors of a region. Its quickest effect is in creating diversification out of the raw material economies of underdeveloped areas. As an area begins to process some of its own raw materials its prosperity increases and it becomes a better market for goods manufactured in other regions of our country. Cheap power is a conserver in another way since the diversification of industry reduces the necessity of a region to mercilessly exploit its basic materials.

For a hundred years we have skimmed the cream of our western and southern minerals, forests, and land resources. Yet today our tools plus electricity, used on a wide scale, can insure that the remaining deposits will continue to enrich the world. The application of cheap power to our forest resources opens up vast potentialities for the creation of plastics, alcohol, and other chemicals. The entire tree can so become a producer of wealth, instead of being one-third lumber and two-thirds waste as it is now.

Today fish canneries discard almost as much value in vitamins and proteins as they process. With adequate research and the application of cheap power, synthetic fibers, artificial leather and many pharmaceutical substances will emerge from the scrap of the fishing industry.

The most important of the basic resources of any region is its soil. Its fertility is essential and electricity plays an important part here also. An almost infinite supply of phosphate lies dormant and unused in the Northwest. Through the electric furnace process developed by TVA, low-grade phosphate shale may be used as effectively in the production of plant food as is high-grade rock under other methods. To work our minerals, forests, seas, and fields we need more, ever more, electric power. The process which started with the first wavering incandescent bulb will, if now permitted to expand, inevitably provide an answer for the economic equality of our South and West. From this will flow the economic and social by-products of electricity which come into being as underdeveloped regions are vitalized. Health, education, and attitudes toward neighbors all improve.

In the South, the people look to abundant electricity to unchain them from a Bourbon and eastern-owned primitive economy. In the West the hope of developing the land and the resources is tied up with expanding the power facilities. In the East the increasing need for electricity dictates the St. Lawrence River project. Yet though all this is incontrovertible, the utility industry will do almost anything to keep the public from considering America's need for cheap abundant power as the issue which they have themselves made it by restricting and attempting to cripple the growth of TVA and other public power developments—anything, that is, short of relaxing their opposition. They see these regional developments as a menace pointing to a future when they will not be able to constrict and control the capacities of whole areas. They feel the menace to their profits and to their old-fashioned system of control over the lives of people in entire regions. They cannot see that TVA is the first example of how this country can truly create "The American Way of Life," a slogan which has fascinated the old-fashioned men for decades.

Yet TVA and other regional projects are just that—a building of all the forces for living.

Meanwhile, as the utility companies continue in the future as in the present and the past, they operate in their own interest and against the public interest. Neither Maine nor Pennsylvania permits interstate connections, which means that their electrical production cannot be used to help other states. Nor can they, in times of shortage, get help from their neighbors. This narrow provincialism is the very opposite of the conception of a national grid or transmission system such as is now in use in England and could well be used in the United States. The national grid permits power-rich areas to pour their surplus into the grid and hungrier areas to draw on an ever firm supply. This practical solution to the problem of achieving an adequate distribution system for the nation's power supply is vehemently opposed by the power lobby. As usual, they see in it only danger for their local monopolies. As they push for the enactment of special privilege laws of their own writing; as they oppose, by fair means or foul, efforts of the public to develop the nation's natural resources, they, the chiefs of the tribes of privilege, stand directly in opposition to the modern needs, to the continuation of the progress already made. The monopolists of the power industry have assumed a tragic responsibility along with their leadership in the fight to constrict America's future. They are—in grim reality—the old-fashioned men.

CHAPTER V

Political Oil on the Fire

Oᴵ is high on the list of resources which a growing world population must have. Oil is basic to expansion of industry, that man-made creation which the rear-guard refuses to recognize as itself an indispensable resource. In place of oil, the world is getting political pressure, designed to procure for the old-fashioned men control of the world's oil resources and the ownership of all the facilities for its production and distribution. The story of oil politics and what they do to hold men back begins where the wells are, in Texas, where oil has been the source of fabulous wealth and power—though not, to be sure, for the vast majority of Texans.

Here is a look at the Texas balance sheet: First in oil and gas; forty-eighth in control of pellagra (malnutrition's prime disease). Texas has 19 per cent of the nation's pellagra. It is thirty-eighth in public school systems; forty-seventh in public library systems. Texas is thirty-third in per capita income. What does all this mean?

A Senate Committee, in its 1949 report issued after an

eighteen months' study, said that the twenty large integrated oil companies now carry on all four main functions
of the industry—producing the crude oil and transporting,
refining, and marketing it. To the Committee this meant
that "The continued concentration of the control of the oil
industry, from reserves in the ground down through to the
tank truck or filling station sale to the consumer, in the
hands of a few integrated companies represents a real
challenge to American ideas of free enterprise and the preservation of small business." The 100 largest stockholders
of Shell Oil Corporation own nearly 90 per cent of the
common stock of that company. In the Sun Oil Company
the figure is almost 85 per cent. Shell is owned by interests
in Holland, England, and New York. Sun Oil is owned by
the Pew Family of Pennsylvania. Other well-known families, not Texans to be sure, have key interests in many companies. Typical are the Harkness, the Flagler, and the
Rockefeller families, which have substantial interests in
the six majors of the Standard Oil group. The Mellon
family controls Gulf Oil. 718428

The Rockefellers, the Mellons, the Pews, and the other
oil kings keep a close watch on their Texas province. If that
state ever got out of the clutches of the oil men and their
henchmen, Texas could, by levying an equitable tax on oil
and other resources taken out of its soil, build and maintain
the finest schools in the world. It could easily have modern
hospitals in every county, highways and farm-to-market
roads, parks, playgrounds, museums, and cultural centers.

Texas might then be first—instead of near the last—of all the states in support of its aged and its dependent children.

Texas is one-twelfth the size of the United States. The largest of its 254 counties is six times larger than Rhode Island. Were it populated at the same density as Massachusetts, Texas would number 145 million people. With room to grow and fabulous riches to grow with, the emergence of Texas waits on projects which will reorganize nature on a scale commensurate with its potential. The attractive, straightforward, and boastful Texans are just the people and have just the land—including the great basin of the Rio Grande, which cries for development—to take leadership in the fight for well-being for a world. That they do not and cannot is largely because of the pervasive and withering political hold of oil.

The hold of the oil men in Texas is symbolized in Dallas by the sign of the Flying Red Horse. Come into Dallas from any point of the compass and the team of Standard Oil Company's flying red horses, which revolve atop the city's highest building, dominates the scene. Dallas and Texas live under that sign—literally.

But the oil men have not been content to control Texas alone. A recent newspaper advertisement reads, "The Flying Red Horse Spans U. S. A.," and though this is, of course, far from true politically, the oil chiefs are behind the seats of the mighty in many states. This is especially so in the South, where the whole region was recently tied together into a political package, better to serve the oil men and their friends of the power companies.

Behind the 1948 Dixiecrat party and their astoundingly flush campaign chest was the familiar pattern of opposition to TVA. In addition, and of first importance to the oil interests, was the shadow of a 1947 Supreme Court decision which held that the "paramount rights in and power over" lands under the waters in the three-mile coastal belt which borders all the states were vested in the federal government and not in the individual states. This legalistic language is more readily recognizable as the tidelands decision. It deals with the submerged lands below tide and outside the inland waters of any state. Under these coastal waters, according to most geologists, are huge oil deposits.

The oil men definitely do not want to surrender control of those bonanzas to the federal government. For obvious reasons, they much prefer the states, with whom they can do business without fuss, feathers, taxes, or back talk. This is, of course, easily seen in Texas, but it is also true of Mississippi and Louisiana, where oil men run the states and select many of their officers. Naturally, the oil chiefs want those tidelands back under state jurisdiction where they can quietly make deals which will permit them to get the most oil out the fastest way—without regard for the future, or adequate payment for the oil they would be pumping so merrily.

The Supreme Court aimed its original decision at California, but the issue took on a heavy southern accent with the realization that it also applied to Texas, Louisiana, Georgia, Florida, Mississippi, and Alabama—all with known or potential oil lands off their shores. In all these states the big oil companies are important politically and intend to remain so.

Should the Supreme Court decision stand, that political influence will not count for much since the tidelands and the conservation and development of the oil and gas in them will be the job of the Department of the Interior of the Federal Government. The oil men have not controlled that agency since the days when one of the oil kings handed Secretary of the Treasury Albert B. Fall a black bag full of money in exchange for a big hunk of the peoples' oil reserves. The oil men do not regard their ability to repeat the Fall routine in the federal government as a sure thing. Therefore all signs have pointed to a revival of the states' rights doctrine, under which good old Confederate banner most of the remaining big oil reserves could be rapidly converted into money and power for the majors of the oil industry. The states' rights banner is an almost ideal set of false whiskers with which to disguise this crude business.

From the point of view of the oil companies the perpetuation of the present malleable governments in the southern states and the changing of the federal legislation on the tidelands are a prime necessity. Therefore the Dixiecrat party has been the instrument by which the Congressmen of the Dixie states were welded into a bloc—not at all for the well-publicized purpose of electing the presidential candidate of the Dixiecrat party but to deal with the main issue in Congress in the future. The oilmen, through southern Senators and Representatives, plan to pass a law in the federal Congress, the gist of which will be to make the nation cough up its resources and deliver them back to the separate states.

The oil men—operating through the States' Rights party—did not elect a President of the United States but they have already won their first objective. Congressmen who supported the Dixiecrats, plus allies from California, now constitute a monolithic states' rights bloc which will be as useful to special interests as it is harmful to the general welfare. In the oil men's battle to capture the tidelands, the new bloc—forged in the 1948 election and already pledged to remain organized—can hope to carry Congress, if not by themselves then in return for benefits to other equally selfish coalitions representing railroads, stockmen, or the ever-present power company opposition to regional development.

All of which has nothing whatever to do with civil rights or social equality for Negroes, opposition to both of which were the only advertised reasons for the creation of the States' Rights party—and the only "fight" it cares to admit. Quite as important to remember as the political implications of this new bloc is the fact that all this happened during a nation-wide shortage of oil. The organization of the Dixiecrats may have been a means of getting more power and profit for the oil monopoly, but the effort did not get the country another drop of the oil it needed, or anything like an adequate program to create liquid substitutes. The petroleum industry has, in the past, been a leader in modern research and its developments were remarkable. Lately its research seems directed less to the creation of synthetic fuel than to synthetic shortages.

The oil shortage of the winters of 1947-1948 and the prospects in the future raise some questions. Most succinctly the Senate Committee on Small Business gave its answer. It said, "There is a mechanism controlling the production of crude oil to market demand (or below) that operates as smoothly and effectively as the finest watch. During the year and a half the committee has been investigating the oil industry, there has never been a real over-all shortage of petroleum. . . . At the time the consumers were feeling the greatest pinch in January and February, 1947, there were 220,000,000 barrels of crude oil in storage, mainly controlled by the larger units, which could have been distributed among independent refineries who were running under capacity."

Obviously the shortage was synthetic. But why create a shortage in this country, geared as its economy has been for many years to oil? From petroleum comes 48 per cent of all America's energy—almost equal the energy derived from all other sources combined, including coal, gas, and falling water. Oil is the chief source of energy in the United States and each year it becomes more important. Nevertheless the shortage occurred—and the oil companies, having created it, had a solution immediately ready, not only for this particular shortage but for all which might occur in the future. They demanded government help to permit them to develop—without interference—the oil of the Middle East. There lie the greatest reservoirs, proven resources of about 35 billion barrels in contrast to America's 22 billion barrels. The Middle East oil deposits could be the richest single jackpot in history for the oil kings. The shortage was a strategy directed toward winning that prize. The Middle East prize will bring not only the fabulous fortune from the oil which pours from the wells, but with it also comes a bonus—domination of the economy of all Western Europe. While little is said in the press about this aspect of Middle East oil, plenty is thought about it in government offices in Paris and London—not to mention Moscow.

Experience gives Paris and London reason for headaches. In January, 1948, our government curtailed oil shipments to Europe by 18½ per cent—due to the "shortage" inside this country. That decision gave Europe a somber and alarming demonstration of the power which possession of the world's oil resources gives the oil chiefs of the United States over the continent's economy. Our throttling of oil exports had immediate effects on Europe —as stalled trains, idle factories, and the shutdown of electric power amply testified. Since the Marshall Plan countries produce only 4 per cent of their oil requirements, 1948's curtailment casts an ominous shadow on their future.

The oil companies and their legislative henchmen were

not at all concerned with what Europe might be thinking. They saw the oil shortage with its curtailment of exports as a beginning of the making of important political hay. "Let us," they shouted, "stop all shipments of oil to Europe from this country. Supply them from American privately-owned properties in the Middle East." If they could win this point, the oil chiefs would have their hands on the Middle East trophy. They won. This was an epic victory for the oil kings, in terms of profit possibilities and political power. They wasted no time exploiting the opportunity. The big companies immediately announced plans for spending millions of dollars in the Middle East fields. Standard Oil of New Jersey, fast on the heels of the government decision, issued a statement which illuminated both economics and politics. Its spokesman said, "We recognize that international trade considerations involve political considerations of the highest order."

It was political consideration and manipulation which gave the oil companies their hold on states and on many Latin American countries. Now political considerations give them the Middle East, with Europe as a long-range objective. No one can doubt that these political considerations have been a sizeable factor in the creation of friction with the Soviet Union, which, conceivably, relished neither United States control of Europe's economy via control of her oil, nor the strong bases which we must build on Soviet borders to defend Middle East oil.

Though the 1947-1948 oil shortage was artificial,

created—according to the Senate Small Business Committee—by the oil companies for their own purposes, its
effects on those who suffered from it, at home and abroad,
were real enough. Its benefits to the oil men were equally
real. In the shortage the oil men found a tool which gave
them, at one and the same time, rich profits, (Standard Oil
of New Jersey earned one million dollars a day in 1948)
from soaring uncontrolled prices (boosted from $1.25 per
barrel at the end of 1945 to $2.65 in the spring of 1947);
a dominant voice in the economy—so dependent on their
oil; and the strongest voice of any industrial bloc in state,
national, or world politics. Seen this way the shortage has
been a kind of cold war waged by the oil companies on the
people of the country and the world. The cold war of the
old-fashioned oil men is far from over. Shortages may
again be used to force us to hand over the tidelands, the
rich unexplored continental shelf, or to stop government
from doing any number of things deemed undesirable by
the oil monopolists.

When the shortage hits again, the fact that you know
that it is not a real shortage but a manipulation will not
help you when the oil tank in your basement is dry or when
your car stands idle in the garage, stalled for lack of gasoline. Nor will your knowledge of the many alternatives
by which the oil industry could have kept you warm and
powered your car make you feel any better if the cry that
America must have Middle East oil has, in any way, been
responsible for the coming of war. The cold house, the idle

car, the laid-off worker, and, perhaps and in part, the war—all will be products of the machinations of an industry more given to getting its way, and its oil, politically than to working the hard way. Conversion of coal and shale into liquid fuel; promoting and developing new gaseous fuels; helping to conserve underground resources and to bring out the oil from the huge reservoirs in the submerged lands—these would be the modern way, the opposite of the destructive techniques and set minds of the old-fashioned oil barons.

James M. Minifie was thinking perhaps of all this when he wrote in the *Herald Tribune* of February, 1948, "There is general agreement that, for hundreds, even thousands of years to come, the United States is in no danger of going dry on liquid fuel." In the face of the facts and the opportunities, there still remains the ever-present danger of a manipulated oil shortage. The world's crying and growing need for a basic resource is subject to the men who own the Flying Red Horse and wear King Esso's Red Crown.

CHAPTER VI

Shortage at the Grass Roots

> . . . for want of a nail the shoe was lost;
> for want of a shoe the horse was lost; and
> for want of a horse the rider was lost.
> —BENJAMIN FRANKLIN

INDUSTRIALIZATION, that application of science and technology, has done more to implement Man's ability than any other factor. No creative living would be possible without its further expansion. Our standard of living in the United States is today as high as it is more because of our development of industrial and scientific techniques than because of our continued ability to grow food or to cut forests. This will be true, in more or less degree, for the rest of the world as other countries industrialize, particularly those countries now so burdened with overpopulation. An important part of the solution for the Chinese complex of overpopulation and low living standards is in the social application of scientific technology—in the mechanization of its agriculture and in industrialization.

In his proposal for "a bold new program," President Truman sensed the meaning of what industrialization and technology can do to create the foundation for a better life for all the world. The President had recognized this fact in another way only a few days before, in his 1949 "State of the Union" message, when he spoke of the necessity for expanding the production of power and of steel. So urgent did he find the need for steel that he proposed that the government go into the direct production of steel if the steelmasters continued in their refusal to expand the capacity of their mills. This presidential declaration marked a radical departure from previous Truman policies, but the decision to make the far-reaching statement was forced on the chief executive by the constricting actions of those who control this most basic of all industries. Taken together, the President's statements on the role of industrialization in the world and the damage inflicted on the nation by the steelmen are seen as two sides of the same medal.

The leaders of the rear guard who hold the world back by stunting industrial capacity apply their individualistic code to the unfettered exploitation of the raw resources from which they make their finished products, refusing to accept responsibility for the conservation of those resources no matter how essential they are to the country or the world. This is the oldest form of industrial backwardness, familiar to all in every colony and indeed in our own South and West. The newer form, so evident in the privately owned electrical industry, in oil, and as the President pointed out so sharply, in steel, is the refusal to expand mills and factories, keeping these purposely to a capacity less than public interest demands so that markets, prices, and profits can be easily controlled. The policies for these industries are uniform, decided by a small group of bankers whose essential interest is to make all the products and services which they control yield assured high profits. The men who operate the industries carry out these policies whether it goes against their grain or not.

When the individualistic interests who so constrict and even destroy our economy and our resources are challenged, they react violently against any constructive developments, however remote, if these have the tiniest impact on their power—financial, industrial or political. In this vein the electrical industry chiefs fight down the development of erosion control, flood control, and phosphate processing because all these are connected with the growth of publicly owned electric facilities which might have an effect on their present or future holdings. The oil companies refuse to develop the tidelands and are loath to encourage the river valley developments because more power derived from water would decrease not only the use of oil, but their political influence.

The private electric utility and the oil companies, with the steel industry, are the trinity which controls the modern economy. As all three hold back expansion in their own industries and as each seeks to restrict national developments which might impinge on its areas of control they hold back the development of the nation and the world.

America's domestic future (indeed its comfort and health, wrapped up as they are in the necessity for pipelines for oil and gas, transport for coal, and material for housing) is certainly threatened by enforced constriction of the steel industry. Regional development, most important key to an expanding America, is menaced. The great Missouri Valley development is dependent on abundant supplies of steel, not only for the structures which must be built to reshape the area, but for the reconstruction of many of its towns and cities into industrial communities. To be successful, MVA must have steel readily available from processing plants in its own territory—free from the monopolistic restrictions which would return to the old collusive basing point system and which in the face of 1949 profits—higher than any since 1929—boosted the price of steel $4.50 per ton in January, 1950.

Nor is the need for more steel any less acute in parts of Europe and Asia where, more than anything else, steel is needed for factories and bridges, for homes and power stations. The need for industry, as the resource by which all natural resources are best utilized, is world-wide and it affects all people, urban or rural.

Industry sounds like cities and factories. In our time it is also food and land—crops and farmers. Where Man brings science and engineering to bear on his food problems, results are achieved. His improved seed goes into better managed lands, where mechanized equipment is the rule. New races and species of plants and even of animals provide better nutrition. Floods are controlled, drought eliminated, and lands are made more fertile by the use of electrically processed fertilizers. Whole regions in the United States have demonstrated how readily nature will respond with huge production to modern methods and technology. But almost everywhere the old-fashioned men who dominate America's industry intervene. The industrial capacity with which to produce steel, fertilizer, farm machinery, and power is held down below the needs of the country.

In this entire country, there is not a single locality with sufficient excess electric power to install one additional aluminum factory. More electric power plants are dependent on the will to expand and on other more concrete factors. The companies which make electrical generating equipment are years behind in filling orders. These manufacturers argue that new capacity would not supply more finished goods unless heavy steel plate, sheet tubes, and pipe were available—which they are not, because of the insufficient steel capacity. No one expands sufficiently; everyone blames the next fellow until the circle is complete. It is a charmed circle which the old-fashioned men have created and it spreads like a blanket over the fire of opportunity for all the people of the country.

There is no room to grow. Expansion is impossible in a world which goes up or down on the decision of a few corporate leaders whose interests are those of an industry and not of the public. Increase in the general standard of living in our country has always been in direct proportion to the building up of industrial capacity. Put another way, the margin of extra and unused industrial capacity is what aviators call a ceiling, and in most major industries the ceiling is at present zero. In the power industry this lack of excess capacity has in the recent past meant not only dimouts, rationed electricity, and inconvenience but a holding back of the sale of appliances and of equipment which might now be producing wealth.

Most of our thinking is in the direction of supplying present needs. The problem goes further. It is, of course, essential to build to meet demands now waiting. For a high standard of living it is equally necessary to promote new demands; new uses and new products. Increase of consumption in home and farm is desirable. Included also is the filling of new requirements for synthetic fuel, the promotion of railroad electrification, new demands for power in industry resulting from further mechanization, and application of electricity to low-grade ores to replace disappearing high quality deposits. All these are tomorrow's needs, already tied in knots by today's shortage of industrial capacity. The consequences of this policy of restricting industrial capacity will be another depression. The United Nations *World Economic Report* of July, 1949, made this clear. It pointed out that only a raising of the world level of economic activity can counter the depression which is occurring even while "the world's supply of goods is still inadequate to meet the requirements of the growing world population."

Today a number of basic industries are tightly controlled by a few producers who determine the size of their industry. The DuPonts, a single family, control not only their own vast chemical empire, but own 23 per cent of General Motors, make the decisions for it, and operate a government unto themselves in which General Motors, United States Rubber, and many other huge corporations are puppets, their size, their prices, and their policies all predetermined on the basis of DuPont's and not the public interest. In some cases DuPont or another of the favored few controls all raw materials needed by its competitors. The result of all this is to constrict the market for the few at the price of lack of opportunities and jobs for the many, whose purchasing power may evaporate as a direct result of high prices and restriction of output.

As a national policy, the antitrust laws have failed to save the country from the situation it is now in. A new and positive approach is essential, fostering and encouraging the existence of margins of industrial capacity. The cost of maintaining extra margins of capacity is not substantial if the capacity margins are modest. Where industry cannot or will not, by itself, stand these costs, it is proper for government to bear them, assuming a share of the responsibility for the decisions which would, by creating new margins of capacity, help to build new markets, create new products, and reduce prices. Until more industrial capacity is built we will live in an era of shortage of opportunity, soil enrichment, and standard of living. These are shortages at the grass roots indeed. All of their effects carry over to our raw material resources.

The United States has the world's most highly mechanized economy. Behind the industrial plant of the country are the natural resources from which are fashioned not only the finished products but the machines on which they are made. Industry consumes a tremendous amount and variety of minerals which, once mined, can never be mined again. Its policy toward those resources is of first importance to every American.

Nearly every item which is required every day so that Americans—poor, rich, near, and distant—may live is inextricably interwoven into the use of natural resources. The supply of winter fuel in the basement is linked to the underground stores of coal or petroleum. The lumber with which I intend to build an extension for my kitchen is tied to a declining and inadequate timber yield from the nation's forests. My wife's trip to the grocer and the prices she is charged for fruits and vegetables, as well as their quality and abundance, make my family table an innocent bystander in the fight which rages over scarce water in the Great Central Valley of California. "No man is an island" when it comes to who is doing what to our national resources, particularly when the fertility of the soil and the supply of water are affected—for these cannot be damaged without a small or large damage to everyone.

Mishandling of resources can never be rectified. As the supplies of the things we need diminish, their prices advance and we live in an era of ever rising prices in just those materials we need most. When the oil, coal, copper, and iron ore are gone, there won't be any more, and therefore the rate of their exploitation and the amount of waste or worse involved in corporate operations are Number One business for the people who will do without these necessities in the future. This is true of the minerals which, once taken out, never will be mined again, but it is curiously doubly true of those resources which are renewable. As the ore is mined out, as the oil is dried up, we must turn more and more to wood and to plants which we can grow to make chemical substitutes and plastics. We will then be using crops not only for food, fuel, and lumber but in place of steel, copper, and oil. If the fertility of the land is impaired, if the watersheds are destroyed, then we are doomed—when we needn't have been.

The relationship between our underground resources and industrial capacity is close and gets closer as the high-grade deposits are exhausted. As natural petroleum diminishes, huge plants for the making of synthetic oil from shale or gas become imperative. As the top-quality iron and copper ores are used up, large factories to process low-grade ores into usable forms become vital. On the surface of the land the tie with industry is equally intimate. The remedy for the exhaustion of the fertility of crop lands is fertilizer, but phosphates and nitrogen require great new factories for their processing. Whether or not America's farmers get the fertilizer they need at prices they can afford to pay should not be left to the seven companies which, according to the Federal Trade Commission, control almost all the phosphate industries. There is even less reason for leaving the future of America's soil in the hands of those four companies which run the potash industry, since nearly all potash is mined from publicly owned lands, located, explored, and test-drilled by the taxpayers themselves—but exploited, without control as to profits or conservation policies, by a favored few. Particularly and emphatically, this group must not be in a position to veto the expansion of the industry on which depends the fertility of the land.

As our natural resources diminish, our industrial capacity must increase or we will remain what we now are—musclebound. Farmer, worker, and every other citizen have a definite and compelling interest in understanding the old-fashioned men who keep us from moving forward and the ways by which they strengthen themselves.

If we are to solve the problem in the next half century, the role and the rights and the ethics of the giants of the corporations must be clearly defined. The private right to a profit cannot much longer be construed to include—or permit—limiting of needed production expansion, opposition to socially important regional development, or wastage and damage to resources. Such a swing could be as good in the long run for the old-fashioned men themselves as it would be for the country and the world. It would put them once more on that road which they trod in the first days of the industrial surge—a time which gave great material benefits to the world.

CHAPTER VII

Customs and Taboos—
American Style

The thinkers who think less of men than of nature are in most part as conscious of their actions as are the men who place private profit above public interest. These men I have described. But there are others who are less conscious of what they do than are the prophets of doom and the corporate giants.

Millions of people live, as their forefathers did, by strict precepts—welded to customs, habits, and traditions, the origins of which have often been forgotten and which, at their inception, may well have been useful and constructive. The needs have long since changed, but the outmoded practices go on, in diverse forms.

The outworn customs may, as in China, take the form of an addiction to ancestor worship and the continuation of practices now harmful but continued out of veneration for those ancestors. In India and other countries, the old constricts the new through taboos which have their origins in religion. These being practiced to the letter, the population is deprived of a chance to properly develop the land or even to eat the food which grows on it.

In many European countries the obstacles to development are tied up with legal custom—long absorbed into the social fabric—which prescribes that the land shall be divided into parcels for each of the heirs, a practice which eventually leads to handkerchief-size patches from which no one can be properly fed. Tenant farming, current in many countries, is the perpetuation of an outmoded economic practice which works havoc on the land. Since the tenant is without any assurance of tenure, he is unable to take responsibility for the land and necessarily permits agriculture to stagnate—seed and stock to deteriorate, and buildings to fall into ruin.

There are many such practices. They are not the monopoly of foreign countries—something done only by people less advanced than we. The United States has its own store of practices based on taboos, traditions, legislation, and social acceptance; and, just as everywhere else in the world, our outmoded customs are acclaimed and defended as great virtues by those who are committed to yesterday and afraid of tomorrow. In this country a landowner residing in a far-away city can clean-cut all the trees on his property, though in doing it he destroys the water source for men and wildlife alike. He can, without being held to account, confine his plantings to crops which are harmful to the land, and by doing so ruin not only his own land but contribute mightily to making dust bowls and barrens of his neighbors' lands. He can, once he has the deed to a tract, strip and gut the land to get at the underlying minerals, leaving gullies and flood-creating ravines behind him.

If he is a stockman, the American can graze as many cows or sheep as he likes on his range, though the effect may be to ruin the grass cover and in this way deplete the underground water table on which farmer and city man are dependent for water to drink, for irrigation, and for industry. The American can build a factory well up on the banks of a stream and proceed to pour industrial wastes into it, polluting it so fish cannot live in it and man neither drink it nor swim in it. And all these are accepted as among the prerogatives of private ownership, blessed by a whole folklore and protected by what is advertised as the American tradition. These so-called rights of individuals—many of them criminal in their effects on the rest of the population and on nature's structure—are rooted in American custom. The group practices which flow from them are under the same umbrella.

Practically all the time both major political parties operate to protect the right of the individual to act in his own interest even when that action is counter to the interest of everyone else. It is only when the nation is prostrate under depression or when the land is in critical danger—when floods or dust bowls threaten—that the two big national political parties act to curb individual excesses and to protect the general interest. At other times, except under such outstanding leadership as that of both the Roosevelts, the two parties are equally amenable to the pressure of the groups who represent the individuals committed to safeguard their unrestricted right to plunder.

The old-fashioned men are well organized into groups— not in the common interest, but in their own. They have strong associations and pressure groups to protect their grazing rights, mining claims, lumbering, electric power, and contracting interests. The list is as long as the number of endeavors in which Americans utilize natural resources for personal gain. When the crisis is acute enough, even the united power of all these pressure groups cannot successfully stymie all constructive efforts. However, in stable times they are too often able to stop any move in the direction of integrating and making better use of the earth's broken floor—as with the repeated diversion of the Missouri Valley development into aimless and piecemeal navigation, flood control, and irrigation works. Most of the efforts sanctioned by the pressure groups are concerned only with flood protection and with the perfection of navigation, neither being an activity likely to curtail their privileges.

What they espouse when they do give their support to a measure is for today alone, instead of for the present and the future together. The old-fashioned men are perennially able to make us the victims of the expediency which they have found so profitable. They stop when they have won a tiny battle for today in their own interest. And custom and property have made them so strong that we have not been able—against their opposition—to add tomorrow's needs to their conception of today's expediency. Only rarely are we successful in writing into law that necessary forward vision which would make of a narrow and short-term palliative a lasting and great victory for all the people. When the United States Supreme Court recently affirmed the constitutionality of a Washington law that requires proprietors of land used for commercial logging to provide for its reforestation, it gave the people such a victory.

The words of the Washington Supreme Court set the foundation for a proper public policy on the preservation of resources. The "inviolate compact" between the dead, the living, and the unborn, said the Court, "requires that we leave to the unborn something more than debts and depleted natural resources. Surely where natural resources can be utilized and at the same time perpetuated for future generations, what has been called 'constitutional morality' requires that we do so."

This was well said, and the opposite of the policy of expediency, the old way of doing only what is necessary for the immediate short run, which always pays off in the same way—in cosmic frustration. A forest is lumber and it is fuel. All the trees can be cut down quickly and some fires stoked and some houses built. But nature, having been disregarded, will react just as callously as did the man who cut the forest. Her answer—brusque and final—will be flood and drought tomorrow in payment for Man's expedient action of today.

But what a profound difference takes place when men see the forest for what it is—not only lumber and fuel, but the source of water, the crown of fertile land, and the domain of varied and infinite insect and animal life. Then Man, using his imagination, applying his knowledge, and teaming his efforts, wins not only more lumber and fuel but, in adjustment with nature, preserves a balance guaranteeing beauty and prosperity far into the future. This is Man's intelligence working in the modern manner, its infantile weakness of chasing the rainbow of expediency outgrown, able to cope not only with today's needs but with tomorrow's problems.

The expedient way is the old way, and it is the expensive way, as is strikingly illustrated by the floods in the Missouri Valley, now the worst in more than a hundred years. The Army Engineers, dedicated over its long history to carrying out the wishes of the expedient men, built dykes to confine the river in much the same way that children, pretending that they are besieged soldiers, build a mud fort to keep out invaders—and to as little purpose. The helpless hundreds of thousands who live along the banks of the river placed their faith in those mud banks which the Missouri River collapsed and disintegrated. The men whose sweat built those dykes wasted their energy. The resources of the American people, so lavishly poured into those walls and ramparts, were gone with the flood. And as the Missouri's muddy waters widened—unfettered and unconstrained—the standing crops on thousands of acres of farmlands were washed away. Topsoil, accumulated ounce on ounce over centuries until millions of tons lay on the valley lands, poured down to the Gulf, the land's fertility going with it, out of reach by Man. The Army Engineers' action and its consequence provide as convincing and catastrophic an example as could be found of the futility of conquering nature on the basis of old-fashioned expediency. What is happening on the Missouri River is typical of the old-fashioned approach to what they call the "protection of our resources"—guaranteed to squander them piecemeal.

It is no accident that this antiquated crazy quilt is, on the Missouri, being patched up by the Army Corps of Engineers. That is the arm of government which the special interests have promoted as the sole instrument by which flood control and navigation are accomplished. The Army—in every country the most conservative of forces— has in return for the support of the special interests consistently protected each of their sacred cows. Flood control can be harmful and navigation temporary and meaningless, unless each is done as part of an over-all basic solution of a regional problem. The Army avoids any taint of such an over-all philosophy. As the agency responsible for large-scale public works, the Army should execute the job, but to do that would cut in on the vested interests of contractors; consequently the Army lets its work out to private contractors.

Legislation which authorizes the projects to be carried

out by the Army Engineers was long ago labeled "pork barrel"—public recognition of the profits for the few, the favors for the privileged, and waste of public funds which is involved in Army activity. And the "pork barrels" get voted each year no matter which party is in power. The cumulative result of the special interests' support of the Army Engineers' "pork barrel" is an American custom as pernicious as any of those which stem from Chinese ancestor worship or Balkan parceling of farms into one-acre plots.

Because the Army Engineers are at present up to their hip boots in a rear-guard action to stop the drive for a Missouri Valley Authority—and so to constrict into their corsets of levees, dykes, and sandbags—America's greatest opportunity of the future, their activities warrant analysis.

CHAPTER VIII

Nature in a Straitjacket

THE Corps of Engineers of the United States Army is an aloof and brass-bound unit of dignitaries. Its gold-bedecked senior officers don't often bother to attend conferences called by residents who have become concerned with what the Corps may be doing to the rivers along which they live. The brass rarely participates in gatherings where civilian engineers and scientists discuss the nation's water problems.

The Army Corps neither explains its plans to the citizenry nor does it deign to argue the merit of its programs. Citizens, civilian engineers, and scientists may propose but only the Army disposes. The corps of Engineers has grown accustomed to its role of omnipotence through the decades in which it has been entrusted by Congress with responsibility for insuring the navigability of the rivers and harbors of the nation.

Accustomed to wielding all authority, the Engineers naturally dismiss—arbitrarily and brusquely—any civilian proposals, especially if they sound like TVA. That disdainful attitude could be expected from the brass toward mere men—but the Engineers are just as unyielding, inflexible, and arbitrary in their dealings with nature. Over the years, the Army Engineers have become cemented to the notion that the way to control a river is to put it into a straitjacket. And any number of floods and droughts fail to convince the men in uniform that nature abhors a straitjacket and will not stay in one even when it is the august Army which has decided that it should. The truth is—though the Engineers will not look at it—that nature refuses to take orders. This may come as a surprise to men accustomed to giving orders but the story of King Canute's try—so similar in intention—has been around for a long time now and the Army might have learned that even a king's authority topples before the movement of water.

Nowhere is the folly of the Canute method used by the Army Engineers, as clear as along the Mississippi and the Missouri rivers. Each year the Army goes through the perennial motions of tying the big rivers into what it thinks will be a constraining and restricting pattern of dykes, levees, and sandbags—and each year the rivers roar down, tumbling over and around the Army's works. Each year the floods get worse, kill more people, destroy more property, and ruin more cropland. One might surmise that somewhere along the line the Army brass would have stopped and taken stock—so many failures, so few successes; conceivably, just one general might have noticed that record and brooded over it, perhaps even considering the ever so remote possibility that the Army's entire conception could be wrong. But instead, the series of defeats inflicted on them by nature have met the old Army answer —more of the same in larger doses. So the Engineers— heedless of nature's forceful objections—build bigger and many more, though unfortunately not better or effective, dykes and levees.

At present the Engineers are having a field day along the Missouri, where they have established themselves complete with plans, contractors, and appropriations. The chief officer of the Army Engineers, General Lewis A. Pick, served notice on the muddy river. "I am going to control all the waters of the Missouri," *Time Magazine* quotes him as saying. This is a large order, in the face of the singular record already chalked up by the Army. In one hundred years of "controlling" the Missouri River, the Engineers have already spent $400 million of public funds on the lower Missouri River alone. Yet the floods grow progressively worse and navigation is sketchy to the point of being nonexistent. Flood crests now rise to all-time highs from Omaha, Nebraska, to the mouth of the river. The amount of dredging necessary to keep the lower part of the river open for navigation has grown to proportions which dwarf every previous earth-moving job from the pyramids to Boulder Dam.

One of the theories to which the brass is most devoted is that a river, once forced into a narrow bed, must thereupon scour out a deeper bottom. The record shows considerable scourings of buildings, farms, crops, roads, and—perhaps because nature thinks a twist of the Army's tail a sly joke —even of the Army's own vaunted works. These have been scoured sometimes right out of existence, to the tune of millions of dollars worth of losses. Scouring does indeed take place but unfortunately not of the river bed. That fills up—and needs dredging day after day, decade after decade.

This Army game is old and its theories have had a full test. The Ohio River has now been fully developed by the Army on the Army's historic plan. The result? The Ohio Valley is today the scene of America's worst floods. 1950 has brought catastrophic floods along the Mississippi River, again underlining the lack of the effectiveness of the Army Engineers' century of work on the "Father of Waters." The Army has also been busier than a corps of beavers in the many other rivers and harbors of the nation. The millions of tons of silt which endlessly pour down these smaller rivers into the harbors might have, along with the floods on the Ohio, Missouri, and Mississippi, demonstrated some of the facts of nature to the Engineers. One spectacular example is the Hudson River, the mouth of which is New York Harbor. Each year enough silt is dredged out of that harbor to fill a string of freight cars from New York City to Omaha, Nebraska, to the never-ending delight of a very few and the never-ending expense of the rest of us.

It all points to one conclusion. While the Army has

failed to build an effective flood control and navigation program, it has succeeded—all too well—in building a merry-go-round the like of which the world has never before seen. On this expensive carousel ride not only the Army but the many contractors who are employed by them to dredge the muck out. The Army sits on its appropriations and whirls merrily; the contractors sit on their gravy boats, dredges, steam shovels, and barges and reach for the brass rings, in this case made of solid gold. But there are other riders on that merry-go-round—the taxpayers— and they are understandably dizzy. The cost of the ride is high, and they are paying for it.

Fundamentally the Army is stuck on its own merry-go-round—and it is stuck traditionally and even legally. By practice and custom it is committed to confining its solutions for the problems of the river to the water inside the river banks. Legally the Army has no jurisdiction over the land and cannot consider that vital factor in planning for the control of floods and of navigation. Perhaps that narrow approach was the best possible within the limits of Man's knowledge in 1833 when the United States Army sent its first engineer, Lieutenant Robert E. Lee (later to be General Lee), to the Missouri River. But a lot of water has crashed over and around the Army-built dykes and the levees since 1833 and in that interval Man has learned that the problem of the river and its floods is also the problem of the mountain slopes, the forests, the ranges, the pastures, and the fields. Man has learned that most of the means to regulate a flow of water lie upstream in the headwaters and not at the mouth. In the century and more which has rolled by since Lt. Lee first saw the Big Muddy, the science of medicine has learned that lesions and sores are often deep-seated, and that a permanent cure for the skin disease can only be effected internally and not by treating the outward symptoms.

Testimony that the Army Engineers are cumbersome, inefficient, and the darling of special interests came from an unexpected source when ex-President Herbert Hoover denounced the Corps on February 7, 1949. Mr. Hoover, intent on governmental reorganization, had recommended that the Engineers be made into a civilian agency. As presently constituted, the Engineers Corps employs 50,596 persons, including 1500 regular Army engineers, 1100 Reserve and National Guard engineers on extended active duty, and 9000 professional civilian engineers.

The former President characterized the work of the Army Engineers as replete with "tremendous waste and duplication," needlessly costing the nation "several hundred million dollars a year." The Engineers reacted to this criticism by deluging the Congress with thousands of protest telegrams. Mr. Hoover suggested that a Congressional Committee might well investigate the source of these telegrams, since he believed that they emanated from contractors and other companies which, in the former President's words, "fear what will happen if the present pattern is destroyed." As indeed the corporate giants might.

To a lesser degree, the Bureau of Reclamation, the Army's one civilian competitor for the control of western waters, is caught in the vise of the same old-fashioned concept. Also lacking the legal authority to manage both river and land resources, the Bureau similarly confines its ministrations to symptoms rather than causes. Primarily the Bureau is charged with the problem of irrigation and all its other solutions for river problems must rest on this narrow base. Flood control, navigation and hydroelectric power production, fish and wildlife preservation, forest renewal, recreation and soil conservation are all part of a single valley problem along with irrigation. Obviously the Bureau structure, attempting to carry out all these jobs, ends up as a pyramid standing on the head of its irrigation. The Bureau of Reclamation tries to get control of great basins by constricting the basic concept to irrigation—the Army does the same thing under the guise of flood control and navigation. In the process each has become a vested interest. Both extend themselves to stymie any attempt to set up administrations of the TVA type, since the basic approach is not a narrow single purpose under their control, but the management of the land and its river as one unit, to be used for many purposes.

The Missouri River is, by all odds, the country's greatest integrated water basin and only an over-all plan and administration can realize its mighty and varied potential. But that administration would necessarily step on the well-nourished toes of the Army Engineers and the Bureau of Reclamation, eliminating single and narrow domination in favor of a more efficient, integrated unit. How the Army and the Bureau react to the threat of losing their control to an over-all agency is now clear.

Before MVA was broached, the contest for control of the Missouri River was in the traditional style. The Bureau of Reclamation fought the Army and vice versa. Their intramural battle came out into the open in 1943, shortly after the Army Engineers announced General Lewis A. Pick's plan for the Army development of the lower river. Reclamation didn't need long to discover that the Army's plan had marshalled some powerful forces to its support. Those supporters should have interested the ordinary citizen even more than they did the Bureau of Reclamation, since the roster provided solid answers as to just who was hoping to get the real benefits of the Pick Plan. The lineup behind the Army Plan included almost all those interests which have stakes in the old-fashioned pattern of privileges for the few. The great network of privately owned power companies quickly recognized that the implications and meaning of the Pick Plan were indeed friendly for them. They saw that the Army program would smother the entire enormous hydroelectric potential of the lower valley. The power companies thought this very nice of the Army and gave the Pick Plan not only their blessing but the support of their far-flung propaganda network.

The railroads read the plan. For them it meant that Missouri River navigation would be no real challenge to their transportation monopoly. Forthwith they rallied sup-

port for the Pick Plan with all their not inconsiderable
might, neglecting no possible ally down to the Pittsburgh
Yacht Club, which was perhaps more interested in keeping
the West geared to Pittsburgh steel than in cruising
yachts up the muddy Missouri.

The contractors, old comrades of the Army, cheered.
They would be awarded the endless and well-paid job of
dredging the river to get sand and gravel to build dykes
and levees which would have to be heightened or replaced
by dredging the river to get more sand and gravel, to
heighten and replace dykes and levees, ad infinitum. The
Army's Pick Plan was obviously a contractor's dream
about to come true.

But the Bureau of Reclamation also recognized some
solid implications for them in the Army's plan and they
were not in the cheering section. To them it meant an iron
curtain erected on both sides of the big river—effectively
shutting them out forever. They rolled with the Army's
punch and countered quickly with an obviously "quickie"
plan of their own, ostensibly designed for the upper
Missouri Valley. Known as the Sloan Plan, the Bureau of
Reclamation plan plumped for a large number of reservoirs on the tributary streams as well as for the Missouri
itself; the stated purpose being to impound water for
irrigation projects, and, incidentally, to develop some
hydroelectric power. The Sloan Plan was thrown together
overnight—less with the idea of developing the Missouri
River than of preventing the Army from perfecting its

claim, based on its navigation program, to all the waters of the Missouri.

Men and women over the country watched the developing conflict between the two agencies with increasing trepidation. Neither of the government agencies was providing an answer in the general interest. The citizens themselves came up with a proposal beneficial to the land, the water, and the people. They, in the public interest, offered a plan for a Missouri Valley Authority, resting on the principles first proposed by Senator George Norris, himself one of the most illustrious sons of that Valley. The MVA idea, like that of its predecessor TVA, is powerful and the two bureaucracies at once realized its dangers to their vested interests. Though for years the Army and the Bureau of Reclamation had hardly been on speaking terms their common fear of an MVA drew them together fast. Only a short while before the MVA idea was proposed, the Bureau of Reclamation had publicly damned General Pick's Army Plan in detail. The Army spokesman had been just as derogatory about the Sloan Reclamation Plan, dubbing one of its great projects impractical dream stuff. But as soon as MVA became a possibility, both agencies dropped all criticism of each other and buried the hatchet pronto. Army brass and Reclamation Bureau chiefs hurriedly assembled in Omaha, and smoked the pipe of peace. The result of their great confab was the Pick-Sloan Plan, a combination of the same Army and Reclamation proposals which had previously been so heartily condemned by each.

The Pick-Sloan Plan is the new Missouri Compromise. Once it is finally agreed upon as the method by which the Missouri River shall be developed, a great hope goes into the discard. The river, its water, and its power will not be used as the great natural force around which will revolve soil programs, resources development, industrial growth— in short a floor for a better life.

These are catastrophic consequences of the Pick-Sloan program and they must be kept in mind. Engineers of the Federal Power Commission have publicly stated that a minimum adequate power program in the Missouri basin would develop 25 billion kilowatt hours of economic electricity annually. Yet the Pick-Sloan Plan callously wastes two-thirds of the potential charted by the Federal Power Commission. Nine million citizens will feel the effects of that waste. The failure to develop electric power cancels out the almost unlimited opportunity for increased industrial development in the Missouri Valley. Specifically it will inhibit, perhaps block, the creation of a great new phosphate industry based on nearby deposits.

This phase of the Pick-Sloan Plan delights the fertilizer and the private power interests for reasons which come up clear in Montana, one of the key states in the Missouri basin, and a state which badly needs both soil and power benefits. The Montana Power Company has made a nice thing of its monopoly of electric power in the intermountain area. Montana Power wants no competition from public power in its domain, and Montana Power interlocks with the Anaconda Copper Company, which is a large producer of the regular commercial type of phosphate fertilizer.

These are the special interests which will benefit from the failure of the Pick-Sloan Plan to develop sufficient publicly owned power. The public interest is disregarded; the whole fertilizer potential is menaced—to the detriment of the businessmen of the region who would set up the processing plants, and of the workers who could work in them. These are on-the-spot losses, but the greatest loss is to the whole country which in this undeveloped rich phosphate area has a real basis for a program that might increase the fertility of the soil of countless farms, which otherwise will slip further and further into sterility.

This is a big price for the nation to pay for the failure of the Pick-Sloan Plan to develop the maximum of the hydro power potential. The effects are obviously not limited to fertilizer. They are so many, piled one on another, that they could cancel out the spiralling upward movement which has every chance of starting with the coming of ample supplies of light and power. The dark shack of the sheepherder in the uplands and the boulevards of the river cities will both be affected. Those cities, proud queens of the river banks, will feel the effects of the Army's enforced electric malnutrition most keenly for the Pick Plan has, true to its straitjacket pattern, provided for not one single power installation along the Missouri River between Omaha and its mouth, an area where ten to twelve billion kilowatt hours might be developed, and a region now woefully short of generating capacity.

Lack of sufficient electric power to support a growing industrial area is in itself critical, but the Pick-Sloan Plan will also result in a shortage of water. Since the first announcement of plans for Pick's flowing navigation channel in the lower river, and Sloan's irrigation projects plans in the upper basin, it has been clear to experts that the amount of water available is not adequate for both uses. Years ago Colonel Jerome Locke proved that there simply isn't enough water in the upper river for both the Pick and Sloan schemes.

More recently, the Hoover Commission has declared that there are "grave doubts" about the adequacy of water for both plans. It pointed out that in addition to the water needed for the Pick-Sloan Plan, about which they had such doubts, it is inevitable that there will also be future upstream requirements of water for a land program, for more irrigation, for industrial uses, and town and domestic use for which no allowance has been made in the Pick-Sloan schemes. One of these demands will be a very large user of water: research is now under way on use of the enormous lignite deposits of the basin for synthetic fuel. If a process is developed, large quantities of water may be required by that single industry in eastern Montana and the Dakotas.

That the Army neglects new possibilities is understandable in the light of its generally old-fashioned outlook. But in the Pick-Sloan Plan it ignores the old as well as the new. The forests, which rule the river and determine whether it will produce flood, drought, or steady flow, are not protected in the Army program. The Forestry Service has, in real alarm, pointed out the total omission of planning for water-crop lands, high in the mountains and at the heads of creeks. The water-crop areas in the highlands are the fundamental storage basins for surplus water.

Though it disregards these natural reservoirs, the Army does have plans for enormous and costly man-made storage reservoirs. All of these are to be located in their private bailiwick, the main stem of the river. At best these huge storage reservoirs are a prodigious waste of money, for the land, properly handled, will store more of the water as it falls and it will release it gradually and do both chores for a fraction of the cost; at worst the Army reservoirs will flood good bottom lands and if the forests above are denuded, the reservoirs will not be effective anyway. They then become a Frankenstein—demanding ever increasing size to contain the increasing floods pouring down from the bare highlands. It all adds up to tragic waste of our land and water resources, lost not only to this generation, but to the generations of the future. And the story of the waste is still incomplete.

Recently the Department of Agriculture highlighted the profligate waste of water of the Pick-Sloan Plan. The Department of Agriculture demanded a conservation pro-

gram for the lands of the Missouri Valley, certainly an
essential part of the protection and development of the
basin. It proposed to hold some of the water back on the
land by means of farm ponds, contour farming, terracing,
stubble-mulching, and similar well-tested practices. Immediately the Pick-Sloan planners protested, refusing to
approve, crying that the land program would jeopardize
previously planned works. Their attitude is that no matter
how conclusively it is demonstrated that the Pick-Sloan
Plan is wasteful, ill-planned, and harmful, Pick-Sloan
cannot be revised. Instead they announced that the Department of Agriculture land program should be scaled
down and slowed down.

In the Missouri Valley, of all areas, conservation is all
important, yet the Pick-Sloan Plan does nothing whatever
about the dust bowl. It proposes no shelter belts and offers
no land practices that will help to solve a problem which
hangs over the Missouri Valley as menacingly as do the
recurring and costly floods. Drought has done even more
damage than flood. In this Missouri Valley alone, the
United States Treasury has paid out one billion two hundred forty-six million dollars in relief, rehabilitation, and
uncollectible emergency loans as a result of the drought
of the thirties. Drought is a Number One problem which
must be dealt with immediately, for dust storms are again
imminent. As recently as June, 1947, the Department of
Agriculture cautioned the nation that a major dust bowl
can develop within five years—and coupled with its an-

nouncement a warning that the new blows, once they come, will be more severe and destructive than those which made the Okies and Arkies national symbols of regional disaster.

To those who lived through those days when they helplessly watched the wind literally tear away the soil from their farms, the dust storms will not soon be forgotten. Some recall it with wry humor, reminiscing about the gopher who burrowed nine feet in the air before he realized that he was still above ground.

Bitter and poignant days came with the dust storms of the thirties. Little wonder that memory of them still troubles the sleep of the people of the Valley—and less wonder that they fear the coming of that morning when the sun again disappears, lost behind swirling clouds made up of the finest topsoil, suddenly broken up into irretrievable particles of smothering dust.

Yet in spite of sad experience and dire forecasts, the Army is promoting a program for the Missouri Valley in which remedial action for the dust storms is delayed until a never-never time described in the Pick Plan as "ultimately." For the leisurely Army this may seem like plenty of time, but for the farmers of the Valley and for those millions who live on their crops, "ultimately," taken with recent developments, can spell catastrophe.

Since the last dust storms, an additional two and one-half million acres have—under wartime pressure—been put under cultivation in the Missouri Valley. More land is now cropped than ever before in history and a good part of this land is in grave danger. Some of those weakened areas have already started to blow away, in spite of the fact that there has been unusually heavy rainfall. The wet cycle may not last much longer and obviously the need for dust-storm control grows more urgent as time slips by. But urgent or not, the Army—following the precepts of yesterday, unaware of the fact that nature's problems can be solved only when all of nature's and Man's purposes are considered together—goes right on its traditional way, building dams that will silt up and become valueless and aimlessy dredging up bits of the 300 million tons of life-sustaining top-soil which pass annually down the Missouri.

CHAPTER IX

Mountaintop to River Bottom

ALL the 500,000 square miles of land drained by the Missouri River is called the Missouri Valley. To say that parts of Wyoming and Montana, with some of America's highest mountains in them, are in the Missouri Valley sounds odd; but it is in these upland forests that the Missouri River gathers its strength and it is on that savage river that all the people downstream in populous Kansas City and St. Louis and on the fertile bottom lands depend for their very lives. What happens to the forests, the slopes, and the other sources high on the top of the range which nurture the river is vital to the downriver residents. The uplands are in trouble. Nine million Missouri Valley people are directly affected. And, as the Missouri Valley prospers or declines, the whole country will be poor or rich, which gives everyone in 48 states a stake and an opportunity.

If you lived in Montana the beautiful, you would almost instinctively know the score. For in Montana, in the headwaters of the Missouri, can simultaneously be seen the great American opportunity and the obstructions placed in the road to its realization by the old-fashioned men. The Anaconda Copper Company got to Montana long ago and has taken out three and a quarter billion dollars of minerals. "Taken out" is the expression, for the entire assessed value of all the property remaining now in Montana is less than a third of one billion dollars. The American symbol for economic poverty is Mississippi, but that state has property assessed at two hundred million dollars more than is all the wealth on the tax rolls in Montana.

Not only the Anaconda, but the Electric Bond & Share, the Union Pacific Railroad, and the great New York and Boston banks which call the tune for the packing companies and the woolen industry—all are part of the web which has enmeshed the residents of the most spectacular and romantic country in America. Many western stockmen, timbermen, and "suit-case" farmers have furthered the looting of the intermountain region. The combination of corporate power and regional selfishness has left little for the mountain men and their children except the scenery. True, there are some jobs available. This one for instance, which was advertised in Butte, Montana. "Wanted —hunters to hunt wild outlaw horses. Delivered dead or alive to Fox Farms." The opportunity is not profitable, though surely it is appealing with its implications of lonely country, unpeopled ranges, and big skies. The appeal is real and makes itself felt increasingly each year as the fascination of the Rocky highline attracts more visitors. But the impact of the lack of opportunity is just as real—though perhaps less obvious to the tourists.

Each year more young people than ever before leave the Rocky wonderland for more prosaic but easier country in which to make a living. For the last thirty years people have been reluctantly abandoning the snow-clad mountains and the high deserts. Until 1940, optimists were saying that the migration marked only a temporary trend due to the prolonged drought. Now the figures are in for the decade since 1940, and in those well-watered years, with the total population of the country gaining steadily, the mountain states lost another half million human beings. Lost each year were one of two young people coming to maturity and nearly all (90 per cent) of the highly trained young people. The college graduates were less impressed by the gay lyrics of the songs about the Atchison, Topeka & Santa Fe than with the inducements offered by General Electric, Westinghouse, and the other big eastern corporations who comb the state universities for the most promising of the students—young engineers, doctors, teachers, and scientists—trained at the cost of states already poor.

Behind them the young people leave a farming population with the country's highest average age—in the newest part of our young America. But the aging farmers have few of the fertile acres which characterize a young and new country. Before them, from the tops of mountains to the mouths of rivers, stretches of wasteland in the making. The watershed, most important ingredient for the preservation of land fertility, is in grave danger.

First to ravish the highline were the "cut and get out" robber timber barons. The waste of the timber has been prodigious, but much worse is the continuing destruction of the mountainsides from which the timber men cut the standing trees. Wantonly and hurriedly the timber barons have cut, burned, and moved on, destroying the leafy vegetation which formed the forest carpet. The rain poured down and the avalanche of erosion started on its way.

The avalanche is felt in the flatlands far down the Columbia, the Colorado, and the Rio Grande rivers and especially in the valley of the Missouri.

The deterioration of the lush food-bearing lands in these valleys which was begun by the timber lords is being hurried by stockmen. They are in the midst of a battle to capture lands under public ownership and to turn these prizes into unrestricted ranges for their own sheep and cattle. On the battle decision hangs much more than the right of a temporary user of a tract of land to determine what he shall do with it. The issue may well be the future existence of the Rocky Mountain area as a place to live in because these uplands are the watershed and the whole western area is in jeopardy. Should the stockmen usurp the hills now under public ownership they will range every possible head of cattle and sheep on them. Once over-grazed, one, two, or three dry seasons on the watershed and the hungry stock will have "grubbed it out"—eaten the grass to the roots.

Then the landslides started by the timber barons will

really roll—breaking loose soil, vegetation, and rocks with ever increasing momentum. Rivulets will cut new channels with every rain. The farmers on the land below will feel the impact even more than now and one day, after enough has rolled down the slopes, after flash floods and the other handiwork of erosion have done their work, the western man will be looking at a landscape as barren as the hills of China—made bleak and sterile by the same process as that which reduced the Oriental hills to desolation.

Romantic and hidden little mountain valleys have been among the very best of the Rocky Mountain farmlands. Between towering mountains lie gems of valleys five, ten, and even fifteen miles in width. Peculiarly they have no streams anywhere on their floors. Over the centuries these tiny valleys have been filled, often to a great depth, with millions of tons of soft water-borne material from the neighboring mountain slopes. On these rich bottoms grew grass so tall the oxen and the horses of the early transcontinental pioneers were often lost to sight in the waving green. In the days when the grass was tall and the oxen and the wagon teams were coming through, the rain which came to these delightful valleys did much good and no harm, for the tall grass took the blows of the splattering drops, bending close to the earth and preventing the cutting of furrows into the ground, draining slowly and effectively without the necessity for a stream. The paradise began to be lost when the first settler began grazing too many animals in this ideal pasture. No sooner had the livestock eaten down the grass cover than the rains began to cut a path out of the valley. Today some of these channels are fifty feet deep and five hundred feet wide and the inevitability is that altogether too soon the beautiful hidden valleys will disappear into the great ravines.

And as the bell of despair sounds for the farmer and the stockmen in the highlands it tolls also for the farmer in the lowlands. The soil and vegetation washing out of the highland valleys must go somewhere. The only direction it can go is down, where it lands with tragic effects which any traveler can see in the valley of the upper Rio Grande. Not long ago the Rio Grande, near Albuquerque, had high banks and a deep channel, a useful auxiliary to a pleasant irrigated valley in high New Mexico. But the millions of tons of earth and sand coming down from the mountain uplands have filled the channel of the Rio Grande. Today even the tiniest flood menaces the entire valley and the people of Albuquerque are in the futile and endless business of building dykes. The dykes, a corset which nature always resists, simply serve to constrict the Rio Grande. The sediment deposited in the river has raised the river bottom nine feet above the city of Albuquerque, leaving the people of that picturesque town a perpetual job— building high dykes so that the river will not flood them, while the river builds up sediment demanding still higher dykes.

The dykes have already destroyed the Rio Grande's usefulness as drainage for the pleasant Albuquerque Valley, with the result that it is no longer pleasant. Thousands of acres have become waterlogged, alkali has come to the surface, and land, irrigated for 300 years by the Spaniards and the Indians, is being abandoned. And the story does not end with the menace to Albuquerque and its wasted valley. For the sediment in the Rio Grande does not all— or even more than a small part of it—stay around Albuquerque; it goes downstream to find a home in the Elephant Butte Reservoir, built by the United States Government to irrigate the excellent land nearby. The Rio Grande has already built up a vast delta of silt above this reservoir. Once-valuable marshlands have turned into marshes. The river's precious waters have been dispersed, necessitating miles of levees and causing perennial spring floods which pose a constant threat to 250,000 people and $400 million worth of property. The process, begun when the mountain slopes were ruined by the timber pirates, is speeding up. It marches on through hundreds of Albuquerques into the lowlands to the mouth of each of the many rivers which drain the great Rocky Mountain empire.

Lands and peoples far away will feel, ever more keenly, the deterioration of this Rocky Mountain watershed. The hills of Idaho control the future for the lush basin of the Columbia River. Whether Los Angeles and Southern California will grow or will wither away, dying of thirst, is now being decided in the headwaters of the Colorado River in Wyoming and in Utah. (The Colorado River is, according to Michael Straus, Commissioner of Reclamation, "the first example of an approaching of the end of a vital indispensable national resource.") Texas, the land where self-sufficiency is a cult, will bake as a result of what happens in the high hills of Arizona and Colorado. And the breadbasket, the rich Middlewest—secure so much of the time—will be successively flooded out and broiled, its fate decided in the snow-clad mountains of Montana and in the majestic Teton Range in Wyoming.

Year by year the deterioration of the Rocky Mountain watershed proceeds. Individual states and many government bureaus have attacked parts of the problem, but none has yet accepted the total challenge from mountaintop to river mouth.

It is not for lack of federal agencies that the Rockies suffer. The Army Engineers, the Bureau of Reclamation, the Indian Service, the Bureau of Mines, the Bureau of Land Management, Fish and Wildlife Service—these and others have a vested interest in the act being played out so fast. None will merge its interest in the general interest—the over-all plan.

Many people are waking up to the inherent fault. Labor organizations are awakening to the connection between their jobs and water. The awakening is rude; a group of aluminum workers is suddenly laid off—the reason, the hydro plants can no longer supply the great amount of power needed for the process. The men see, with the finality of reality, the connection between their jobs and the development of a watershed. Farmers, once concerned only with how much they could plant, are forced to concentrate on reclaiming fertility from barren soils while 65 per cent of the country's phosphate supply lies unused in Idaho for lack of power with which to process it. And the knowledge that Anaconda Copper, the corporate giant astride Montana, owns much of the phosphate is no less sobering than the fact that its corporate blood brother, the Montana Power Company, blocks the development of the Missouri River.

People are waking up for many reasons. Industry which would develop the West and so provide opportunity for the youth at home is not permitted to get a start. Eastern railroad interests with their discriminatory freight rates share the blame. Feeling grows more intense. The *Rocky Mountain News* uses its entire front page to announce "Western States Battle East." The *Denver Post* shouts "Eastern Monopoly Is Challenged." The reason for this current skirmish? The Intermountain States have always been forced to ship their wool to Boston—the country's woolen center—for scouring. Now, prodded by poverty, the mountain men have decided that this business of shipping burrs, ticks, and field dirt must stop. They will build their own scouring plants and they will clean their wool before it starts for Boston. Eminently sensible though this approach is, it pleases the Bostonians not at all. "Preposterous," they say—such a project couldn't be carried out by the people of a "tumble-weed state." Long injured and now insulted, four states have combined to put the easterners in their places.

There have been such challenges before. But the states on the highline have continued to remain company domain, colonial outposts for big eastern corporations. Some of the rebellions against the masters of mining and power and transportation were put down summarily. Others were perverted by politicians, elected because they were eager to fight Anaconda and the other corporate giants, but only too friendly with them once they were in office. Some were frustrated in subtle ways, as happened in the West's drive to save the big Geneva Steel Plant in Utah. When the war ended and this big plant was shut down, the entire West demanded that the mill be made the basis of a steel industry supplying the West's peacetime needs. The eastern steelmasters were unmoved by the indignation of westerners until it became painfully obvious to Pittsburgh that a maverick of western industry was ready and eager and able to take over the Geneva Plant and produce steel. That threat brought the titans into the picture in a hurry. When the smoke had cleared United States Steel owned Geneva at 20 cents on the dollar of its original cost. In moving in to stop competition, big steel revealed how smooth working are the relationships of monopoly with that large number of western politicians who locally and in the nation's capital prepared the way for Pittsburgh's steelmasters.

Big steel, now firmly in control, has since given the West another and somewhat contemptuous demonstration. The discriminatory freight rates which the West has tried for so long to abolish can easily be changed when it is to the benefit of United States Steel. Freight rates for products made of steel were promptly lowered, and by a process as understandable as it is unique the new low rates were confined entirely to those products moving from the steel mills owned by United States Steel. Simultaneously Utah has discovered that Geneva's presence in that State has meant almost nothing to her people. United States Steel ships the output of that great plant to its own subsidiaries outside the state's borders. Utah still must scrabble to get the steel she needs.

As all these old-fashioned architects—the mining and the lumbering barons, a neglectful Congress and vested bureaucratic interests, the industrial, the utility, and the financial monopolies, and the short-sighted cattle and sheepmen—push their plans for famine and waste on him, the mountain man stops to take stock. His is still a lovely country. He looks at the big winter sky with a love that a city dweller can only faintly imagine. His philosophy has been shaped by this jagged skyline, the mountain spring, and the roaming bear. His outlook is uniquely fitted for a free man, carving out of his rugged environment the means to live. With the watershed ruined, the means disappear and the outlook of the mountain men will change.

Signs of that change are already visible in the south-western high desert where failing hope of irrigation has given way to the creation of a tourist mecca.

The West, from high desert to glacier, is beautiful and the westerner is proud to have an ever increasing number of tourists come to see its wonders. But it is one thing to be proud of your home and to show people around it. It is quite another to be the doorman at Harold's Club in Reno where a Coney Island economy is already in full sway. Coney Island is not the paradise for which the mountain men hope. They do not visualize themselves in the role of old men and women whose children, grown prosperous in the East, come back in the summertime to visit them at the dude ranch where they work.

It needn't end up that way. Any time we want to take a hand at the job, the Missouri River (biggest factor in restoring the West) can be recreated. Can be, that is, if we hurry—for nature won't wait on us forever.

The question is—will we, as a nation, do something about it? And on that answer wait not only those people who live in the Rocky highlands but the millions in the flatlands bordering the Missouri River—a valley in worse shape now than it was when the homespun poet wrote his thumbnail picture of it.

> Where sand is blown from every mound
> To fill your eyes and ears and throat;
> Where all the steamboats are aground,
> And all the houses are afloat.

Some years the basin of the Missouri River is dry and parched. The corn, wilted and stunted, then stands stark and barren on the wasted fields. Mile on mile, the burned stalks are testimonials to the fact that farmers have, once more, wasted seed and toiled in vain. The burned fields testify, in mounting crescendo, to the need for modern management of the land and water, management which would avoid this catastrophe. The drought years speak one stanza in the saga of needless disaster; the great floods tell another—even more dramatically. The 1947 flood of the Missouri River was tragic emphasis on the mistakes of the past and present, and prophetic warning of the needs of the future.

Only a little more than two weeks before this great flood, Army Engineers had sensed danger to a levee near St. Louis. As usual, they leaped to do the expedient thing, doubly necessary now because they had not earlier done the important thing. The Army rushed in to attempt to create a wall strong enough to stand against the rising river. Day and night the Army toiled frantically to save the levee—to keep the now inevitable flood waters away from the doors of the people.

But flood waters are generated in the mountains where there is as yet no effective control and, once the surging flood starts down, it is too late to undertake preventive action. The waters rose higher and higher—faster than the exhausted levee workers could pile the sandbags. Inevitably the levee gave before the torrent, and, as though providing a symbol for the whole of the futile Army system of Missouri River flood control, immediately fanned out and deepened around a truck belonging to the Army Corps of Engineers. The water mounted over the running boards, poured into the cabin, swirled above the vehicle, and finally completely submerged it.

A symbolic scene indeed. Along the 2500-mile stretch of the Missouri River, broken and suddenly stranded communities were the rule. Expediency was demanding its extortionate toll once again.

The flood struck farms, villages, and cities. It rolled down on Des Moines, Iowa, located on a big tributary of the Missouri River. Block after block of the city went under water. The factories where men earn their living were shut down. The homes where men raise their families were washed out. The water poured down the Des Moines River, and onto and over the city of Ottumwa, leaving 8000 people homeless, their houses reduced to sticks of wood—disappearing in dirty whirlpools.

Far below, the parent rivers—the big Missouri and the mighty Mississippi—joined their flooded torrents. Mark Twain, in his best pilot days, would have had difficulty in finding the Mississippi channel. St. Louis, just below the confluence, felt the impact. Tracks, roads, and highways were under water to the north of the great river city. In that section the factories were closed down by the waters. The rising Mississippi started up the city's front steps in its famous downtown area.

Over the entire course of the Missouri, the water, inside and overflowing the banks, was a dark and muddy brown. This was the "Big Muddy," grown bigger with flood and muddier with millions of tons of topsoil, turned now to menacing, churning mud.

All along the river, highways—normally paralleling the river bed—now sloped down to the water and were lost to sight. Bridges, though still in place, led to nowhere but to more water. Bits and pieces of levees remained only as symbols of blasted hopes.

The magnificent locks and dams built by the Army quickly lost their majesty. Water flowed over and around and about them. This must have been a frustrating picture to that greatest of all builders of navigational dams, Brigadier General Lewis A. Pick, Chief United States Army Engineer, and joint author of the Pick-Sloan Plan. Pick himself described the picture in these words: "I could see nothing but water; in some places it was 25 miles wide. I never felt so ineffectual in my life. . . ."

Yet the flood could have been foreseen; it need never have happened. Nature, which was responsible for the rainy season, had also provided a system for checking floods. Both factors were there to be reckoned with. Forest lands and prairie grasslands hold the moisture. Roots retain the soil and keep it from floating away. Had the Army protected and improved that natural system the floods would have lost their virulent punch. But the Army had concentrated downstream on the river. It had no time for, or interest in, the management of the lands. Thus it came about that too much timber had been cut, that marginal prairie lands had been plowed up, and when the rains came, they were no longer held. More water and still more water began to run off. Furrows and ditches became a million tiny rivulets. The rain continued down a drop on a drop and the million rivulets poured into little streams.

The little streams with the beautiful names—the Solomon, the Loup, the Nishnabotna and the Little Sioux, the Elkhorn, the Osage, and the Little Blue—all rushed their load into the tributary rivers. The rivers discharged their heavy burden of raindrops and topsoil into the wide Missouri. Yesterday's rainstorm was added to today's downpour and when all the waters flowed together it was a mighty flood and the Army's downstream works had done nothing to prevent it. Their elaborate dams and levees could do nothing to stay it.

In the State of Missouri the flood had washed over a total of 1,409,000 acres of farmland. In Iowa at least a part of the topsoil from 25 per cent of the farmland was gone. R. H. Musser, regional conservator at Milwaukee for the United States Soil Conservation Service, estimated that the flood had caused $500 million damage and had washed away enough precious topsoil to cover 325,000 acres to a six-inch depth. The rollcall of damage for this flood on a part (not all) of the Missouri was read by Mr. Musser: soil loss, $283 million; crop loss, $188,606,000; urban damage, $17,415,000; damage to highways and railroads, $9,490,000.

The floods have receded now and much of the visual

damage is gone; the smashed homes and factories are rebuilt and housewives have scraped the dirt from their homes. The parlors are again spotless and the frame houses gleam once again with characteristic white paint. But housewife, worker, factory owner, and farmer are not at ease. They know the floods will come again—until and unless the Missouri Valley gets scientific management which begins high in the range and goes down through to the river mouth, and includes the land and people on the whole watershed. The dismal certainty of recurring floods, and the knowledge that a known method exists to curb them to stop erosion and the water wastage, combined to evoke from the *St. Louis Post Dispatch* the big question of the flooded victims: "How long will it take America to learn a lesson that all can see in the Tennessee Valley? What are we waiting for?"

CHAPTER X

Men and Nature

Men, my brothers, men, the workers, ever reaping
something new;
That which they have done but an earnest of the
things that they shall do.

—ALFRED TENNYSON

THE "lesson that all can see in the Tennessee Valley" includes two very important factors. The first is that TVA represents a new, modern, and useful form of social organization. The second is that TVA's achievement is part of a basic revaluation of the relationships of men and nature.

For many generations Man has, of course, had an astonishing capacity to manipulate nature. This capacity he has called his "conquest of nature." But conquest is a delusion; no victories have been won by storming nature. Two thousand years ago Horace wrote "You may expel nature with a pitchfork, but she will always come back again." Nature is not conquered when the forests are denuded. She simply refuses to perform, and drought and flood are consequences. And this has been true in every field where we claim domination over nature. The whole idea of conquest of nature is old-fashioned, born of ignorance.

We are just learning that adjustment to nature is the only method that can work. The relationships among plants, animals, and Man are never satisfactory unless all are in harmony. Harmony with nature is a complete process. It calls for adjustment to the whole—to nature's recurring seasons, tides, and currents, to its surprising variables, its moods of storm and calm, to its inert forms as well as to the living matter which surrounds us. We can understand, if we try, all these myriad interdependencies and, working with them, manipulate those which are assets and neutralize those which are dangerous.

Total adjustment is a new idea. The old idea of conquest of nature still dominates in most of the world. It is all too evident in the overplanting and overplowing and bad irrigation practices on the very land we need for growing the food on which to live. "Conquest of the drought" was accomplished in this old-fashioned way, and nature's answer has been and still is—soil erosion. The worth of conquest is equally obvious in the handling of our water supplies. Though as essential as the air we breathe, we continue to handle our water sources as though they were independent of the rest of nature. Our underground stores of water grow less, while floods, once looked upon as catastrophic, are accepted as inevitable—almost as scheduled events for which we maintain permanent disaster relief organizations. We have conquered the land and we are victorious over the water. Understanding neither, we fail to understand the meaning of these victories. A few more generations of continued conquest and we will have neither croplands nor water supplies.

Failure to see nature in any terms but those which govern a man's own lifespan; refusal, for reasons of quick profit, to use what knowledge is available; and lack of knowledge about the effect on nature of Man's discoveries—all these have contributed to perpetuate the old-fashioned idea of conquering nature.

Adjustment to nature is the new concept and it is far greater in scope and majesty than the old idea of conquest. As we go up this newly discovered path we will restore and enhance nature's beauty, enriching our highest form of expression. Science, religion, poetry, and art all partake of nature's inspiration. Whether old or new, whether in our own Missouri Valley or in Africa, concepts of nature pervade all manner and types of culture. Tomorrow's spiritual life will draw on natural beauty and value in increasing measure as adjustment to nature becomes the guiding precept of men everywhere.

Cultural enrichment is inherent in adjustment to nature. Adjustment will also provide increasing supplies of food and of all material resources. It will change human institutions. Human beings and human societies are not created by machines. They too are plants that grow and must be tended and nurtured inside the whole of nature. Material resources and social organizations have always developed together. Almost always the organization has evolved as an essential to assist in securing food. Only a minute number of resources can be obtained by individuals working alone and in isolation. When men team together in social organizations, they achieve an ever higher efficiency of utilization of resources and expand the number which they can use profitably. As the level of social organization improves, many things which were of no use before become resources. The Negeb desert in Palestine was of no value to the nomads. It is extremely valuable to the Israelis, because their social organization will enable them to utilize its possibilities as fertile and irrigated land.

Nowhere can natural resources be evaluated as materials separated from the social organization of the people who are to use them. The human resources of social organization, knowledge, skill, and intelligence are the resources of "mind." As they develop and improve they steadily become more important in relation to the resources of "matter"—the raw materials secured from plants, animals, and minerals.

As we move into the future, "mind" rather than "matter" becomes the dominant resource. The organization of human beings and the utilization of knowledge, skill, and intelligence move into the top rung in resource problems. The evolving new forms of social organization begin to appear.

Watersheds are slopes which shed the rains and the melting snows. The rain comes off the slopes in rivulets, brooks, and streams, merging finally into a river which runs through the lowlands and out to a lake or the sea. From the top of the slope to the mouth of the river is one integrated region where the river dictates the flow of life, supplying water and providing a high road for navigation. The water is key to the land and both merge into one problem. As our knowledge of the value of adjustment grows, we necessarily form our social organizations on a scale big enough to deal with the problem on nature's terms. This was the striking innovation which marked the inception of the TVA. It was a great advance in social organization and in tune with the needs of tomorrow.

Adjustment to nature's impersonal physical forces and the taking of inspiration from its beauty are only part of the whole. Adjustment to nature includes hills and rivers and wood and fish certainly—but also and paramountly, adjustment to Man as part of nature, which he most certainly is. No one will argue against the idea that Man is part of nature, but over the centuries Man has honored that conception more in the breach than in the observance. Almost every person has so far forgotten his relationship with nature that he unconsciously dissociates his arts, his economy, his institutions, his complex of relationships, his desires, passions, and his prejudices from the rest of pervasive nature.

All of Man's institutions and efforts are the products of his intelligence, completing a natural cycle which began with nature's creation of Man's intelligence. Seen this way, adjustment to nature involves not only the use of intelligence to guide and pilot physical forces, but the utilization of that same natural force of intelligence to harmonize Man's own scientific, social, economic, and ethical forces— for all these are, as they have always been, part and parcel of nature's pattern.

As his intelligence has developed, Man has moved closer to an adjustment with nature. In his progress toward natural harmony, he has started up a road which will inevitably lead him toward more democratic social organization and a creative life for every individual. It is all part of a single process, essential to building up old resources and creating new ones. The process creates the need for its own form of social organization. In TVA the new form was seen clearly and almost everywhere—in India, in the Soviet Union, in Mexico, the United States, and other countries—men are also organizing into modern teams to cope with nature, before which the individual is helpless. Only the group, through its specially organized teams, can do the job and the team is the universal answer—a natural and evolutionary step which permits the expanded use of Man's unique capacity to observe, remember, record, compare, analyze, define objectives, and devise operating plans. It enables him to execute those plans in his own interest, and to manipulate the forces of nature to fulfill his aims.

The team embodies strategic planning and execution which bring every aspect, every resource of nature into one coordinated plan. It is action not only to stop a flood or to halt erosion but to create new values in nature, new growth for Man. When you cut this pie there are many new slices. The new pie is bigger, its great size made possible by the creation of values which never before existed, values which pay not only for the costs of the prevention of flood and soil losses, but which yield a most important and vast surplus of cultural improvement and satisfactions.

The team plans. Its plan must consider the effect of its proposed actions on the interrelationships of all nature, not only for a short interim period, but far into the future. This kind of a plan, full of the realities of the space in which it operates and of the scale of its endeavors, is not— like the Pick-Sloan fiasco—a sheaf of papers replete with dry words, numbers, and structural drawings. Plan and execution are intertwined; an intimate, never still, ceaselessly active relationship exists between them. This is no plan for conquest but a meshing with nature's own dynamics, embracing the impersonal as well as the throbbing personal individuality. Dynamic planning is attuned to the process of constant change presented in all nature.

The planning and execution of plans for development in a great region such as the Missouri Valley cannot be done effectively by remote control or by edict. It is a full-time job, operating every minute throughout the twenty-four-hour day, and no legislative body concerned with thousands of other matters can do it. No executive branch can do it for the same reason. The responsibility comes to rest —as it should and must—on the team organized for the job. Once the elected branch of Government has outlined the tasks, formulated the objectives, defined the responsibilities, and authorized discretionary power the team, specifically chosen for its competence and integrity, takes over. They perfect the first big over-all plan. Obviously none but the team can make the continuous adjustments and readjustments necessary to meet the changing conditions of each day while preparing for those even greater changes which close observation indicates will be necessary to meet the exigencies of some future date.

In these projects where Man is involved with nature in its manifold aspects, the on-the-spot team has particular importance, for nature is full of moods, changes, and outbreaks. The rains may come, bringing floods; the landslides may start down the mountainsides, and nature may have sounded no note of warning for either. Nature has always been variable and men, alone or in groups, have over the centuries developed some capacity for instantaneous action to meet sudden onslaughts. Praiseworthy though this capacity for quick judgments and actions is, it represents only the technique of expediency. The boy with his finger in the hole of the dyke has been remembered for saving the town. He acted quickly and courageously but differently from the modern team, which combines action to prevent calamity in the future with a capacity for meeting present emergencies. The modern team does not spend its time looking for holes in dykes or piling sandbags on levees. It seeks, by a study of the probabilities of nature's onslaughts, to prevent the necessity for either. Its action in the present is designed to guard against the next recurrence of damage. Equipped, able, and ready to provide relief for the victims of a present flood, the team is nevertheless involved in continuous and dynamic adjustment and manipulation of nature's forces to avoid floods.

In the old pattern of conquering nature it has been fashionable—just as it has been expedient—to see only that face of nature which is unfavorable; the floods, the earthquakes, storms, and the droughts. Modern Man has looked harder and seen much more. He has found that nature has myriad favorable aspects which he has never before utilized. The team seeks out these assets and, by causing the favorable factors to work together in harmony, tremendously expands their value to Man. This expansion is not only what we know as "conservation"; it is much more, involving the discovery of new resources and the organization of them for Man's use.

The team, in this new form of social organization for regional reshaping, develops special skills in planning, building, and operating great projects in the public interest. Those are the skills most needed by the world—which explains why TVA alumni are in demand nearly everywhere. It is no accident that a TVA alumnus is engineering the Jordan River Valley Project; that Ceylon urgently requests a loan of a TVA executive; or that David E. Lilienthal headed the Atomic Energy Commission. The

TVA experience developed and sharpened a new skill in every team member. This planning and executing of a large program which will affect all human and natural resources is a new vocation and a great one. Nor is it limited to a select few, born with native talent. This modern skill is technical and can be acquired by training and experience. Here and there a remarkable person, such as David E. Lilienthal, may well be born with a special aptitude for heading a team to remake the planet, but many people can, through training and experience, acquire the technical side of the job. As a technique, the art of mending a world is not much different from mending a watch or healing a sick body. You have to know how to do it—and it can be learned. Enough Americans have already learned it to staff the team for the Missouri Valley.

What then indeed "are we waiting for"? It isn't only that we have the example of TVA; other important things are involved. We can and we must reclaim and reshape this great area in the Missouri Valley now, preventing the floods and expanding Man's opportunity for creative living. And in that "we must" lies the greatest urgency. For the old-fashioned men and their old-fashioned damage have left us no alternative.

We do not have the electrical generating capacity that we need; steel-making facilities are adequate only for the America of a decade ago. Farm machinery and fertilizer facilities are no better. Not only these industrial resources but gas, oil, lumber, and ore are inadequate to meet the requirements of an expanding population and a higher standard of living. Water shortages threaten town and country alike.

An America which counts on a great future cannot have it unless we get on with tomorrow's job today—unless we embark on an immediate program of expansion of our resources and the reshaping of our areas as a cardinal plank in the platform of national policy.

America's situation is not now the same as it was as short a time ago as 1940. Since then we have used up tremendous amounts of our resources. It is imperative that these be replaced, that new resources be found and worked. The job must be done speedily and without waste. Only one area in the country is big enough by itself to provide our major needs and that is the great Missouri River Valley. Its size and its location are but its basic foundation, for the Valley contains unexploited resources which can support expanded agriculture and industry. It offers an integrated region where the electric power, water, and the transportation necessary for large-scale effort are potentially available. And all these are the essentials without which the country will stand still—or go backwards, as indeed the ten states of the Missouri Valley are doing.

Montana, Wyoming, North and South Dakota, Nebraska, Kansas, Missouri, Colorado, Minnesota, and Iowa —an important section of the United States—are losing population (North Dakota lost a quarter of its population between 1940 and 1947). Only Kansas balanced its losses of vigorous young people and families moving out with new settlers.

In the fifteen years between 1930 and 1945, one of every ten farms disappeared. Some went into larger holdings, but cropland actually harvested decreased by seven per cent. Ninety thousand farmers gave up in these years and in 1945, a most prosperous year, the value of all the farms and farm buildings had decreased by a quarter—a loss in value of $2½ billion.

Industry looks even worse. In the glory year of 1929 there were only 20,000 manufacturing establishments employing 600,000 wage-earners in the entire vast region. In 1939 the figure had dropped to 17,000 and 120,000 fewer workers had jobs. Gains from war industry reversed the trend and raised hopes, but these are illusions fast being shattered.

The Missouri uplands are the scenic wonder of the West. Here are Yellowstone and the other great national parks. Birds, fish, and game vie as attractions with forests and an infinite variety of wild flowers. Beauty still lives here, but drying up of ponds and waterways and pollution of streams are destroying the birds and the fish. Clean-cutting of forests is ruining the timberland. Overgrazing is jeopardizing the open range.

The tragedy of this ruin and waste will touch everyone. One half the nation's wheat and rye, one quarter of the sheep and horses, one sixth of its cattle and hogs come from here. The tragedy is all the deeper because the Missouri Valley is still a storehouse of undeveloped resources despite the fact that $6 billion in gold, silver, copper, lead, zinc, and coal have been taken out.

Still untouched lies one of the richest deposits of phosphate on earth, 90 per cent of the phosphate ore in the United States, more than half the world's supply. In one Valley state alone, North Dakota, is a trillion tons of lignite coal, enough to meet the nation's fuel needs for 6,000 years. Montana has 400 billion tons of lignite and bituminous coal deposits. Eight hundred and fifty million tons of manganese line the Missouri River from Pierre, South Dakota, to the Nebraska border, solid bluffs of manganese-bearing rock 40 feet thick.

To a nation wailing the loss of its resources this should be a call to action. The production of synthetic gasoline from Colorado, Montana, and Wyoming shale and sand; the abundance of high-grade mineral fertilizers in Idaho and Montana; iron, clays for aluminum, coal, manganese, and chrome—all point the way to an increase in the supply of resource products and a lowering of their costs.

But the development and use of any one of these essential resources is tightly bound up with the conservation, development, and use of others. Water is essential for power, power for gasoline refining, water for synthetic fuel production. No gains can be made on a wide front except by recognizing interdependencies, the greatest of which is the Missouri River, which touches all resources and all the people. And no gains will be achieved unless adjustment with nature and modern social organization are made possible by political action.

CHAPTER XI

Political Bridgeheads

The legitimate object of Government is to do for the people what needs to be done, but which they cannot by individual effort do at all or do so well for themselves.
A. LINCOLN

BEFORE the Missouri Valley team can come into play political decisions must be made, and in a democracy these involve every citizen. The political decision which differentiated the TVA venture in planning from every other so-called American effort at planning was wise, and in that political wisdom lies the reason for TVA's success. The TVA team, a functional group trained in a hundred specialities, was given a carefully defined job to do. That definition was the first step in wisdom. The people next handed the team the entire responsibility and authority for the job. In this way the team was enabled to exercise its full judgment. Having delegated an exclusive trust to the team, the wise political decision implemented the task, providing the elements necessary for achievement—the money and the tools. The President and the Congress had done a notable thing in a democratic way. The TVA team started its run with a green light, a modern car, and they knew exactly where they were going and why. The result was a landmark in progress. As yet it stands alone in the country. The people and their representatives have provided no other team with all these requisites, without which success is impossible. The development of the Missouri Valley waits on similar political action.

In the nearest future a team empowered by the Congress to get the whole job done must set up the necessary instruments in the Missouri Valley, in order to meet national and international needs, present and future. Only if we do this will this country be in a position to unbind its muscles. To sit still now is to let not only an opportunity but an epoch slip away from us. To bring to bear the beamed power of our intelligence in a forward drive now will win that epoch and begin the reshaping of the Missouri Valley. Not only will the physical features of that huge region be reformed, though surely that is challenge enough. The reshaping of the individual person will begin.

Each of those individuals, helpless now before the savagery of the river and the ruin of the resources, will remain incapable of constructive action because no teamed will, no teamed plan, no teamed action was or is yet at work. To free the individual of the Missouri River Valley requires a plan, a big one. The scale and the perspective required for such a plan cannot come from expediency. It can only come from the teamed use of intelligence. With such a plan in effect the individual will start on his way to being in tune with nature, able to build institutions and personal relations which will make living an harmonious experience instead of the bickering and war-creating frustration that it now is so much of the time. MVA, like its predecessor in the Tennessee Valley, is the type of project needed throughout the world. To undertake it—and to assume responsibility for helping other countries with their similar programs—is to put our shoulders to the wheel of the world's work, to become leaders in creating a way of life in which abundance is but the material vehicle on which free and independent individuals ride securely and optimistically.

Though the smokescreen of press propaganda and radio publicity still obscures what the American people really think about teamwork and regional reshaping— both important trends for winning abundance—every now and again the artificial fog lifts and we get a clearer picture. November, 1948, was such a time. The presidential election swept away the notion that the people of the country were enthusiastic for a return to the tribal chiefs' version of "the good old days." The majority of the people voted, not so much for a candidate, as for the modern approach of which they had seen the beginning under F.D.R.'s New Deal. After the Truman victory those very pollsters who had so blithely said that Dewey and reaction were a sure thing found themselves taking new polls to discover why they had been so wrong. The questions they asked were designed to get answers which, though they might be unpalatable to vested interests, would bring out the truth.

In this framework the *Fortune Magazine* poll asked a pertinent question: "How do you feel about large-scale public power and flood control projects like the TVA and Bonneville Dam in the State of Oregon? Do you think it has been a mistake for the government to operate projects like these or do you think they have been a good thing for the country?"

The pollsters received this revealing answer:

A good thing	76.5%
A mistake	7.0%
Express no opinion	15.5%

Elmo Roper, who conducted the poll, commented, "The principle of TVA is now firmly imbedded in American thinking. . . ."

Since the result came after fifteen years of propaganda designed to convince Americans that TVA is synonymous with socialism, communism, and dictatorship, it must have been a big surprise to the utility interests and to the other privileged gentry. However displeasing it was to them, to the rest of us the answer was another demonstration of the great reason for optimism which is inherent in the future, since it shows that people generally—and not only in the organizations of labor and the farmer—are prepared and want to adopt new methods, to undertake new forms of social organization.

Meanwhile American political thinking and political patterns are still woefully inadequate for these great tasks. In all areas of activity our political life is characterized by indecision and faltering.

Fascist dictators thrive on the doubts engendered by the backtracking of representative government. Again and again they have come to power on the wings of their Lorelei song; representative government is too slow, not capable of acting. Yet no sooner does a Hitler or a Mussolini disappear into the ashbin of history than another strong man turns up—always building up his strength by contrasting his own ability for quick decisions with the picture of the chaotic and stumbling actions of representative government.

This can change only when the majority of the people see, emerging from the new great objectives, intimately individual benefits as well as cosmic advantages. Once this is seen by a majority of the people, the weakness of democratic government and its hesitations—the fatal defects—will be dissolved by the fresh breeze of vigorous action. In place of private corporation pressure will be public pressure, sparked by the groups of the population whose special interests are clearly involved in the progress of the whole world and the whole country and not in a deal for a quick profit.

If this comes about rapidly we will get wise political decisions made by a representative government which understands and acts promptly to clearly define a great social and natural objective. That revitalized government will act promptly to set up a team of competent, imaginative, and adventurous people equipped with the tools, the authority, and the money to create the MVA and to achieve other great goals desired by the people.

Once these teams are in the field we can leave to them the question of method. Properly equipped technically and with a vision of the social and biological meaning of their actions, they can decide which method would be best and which phase of the many-sided development needs greatest emphasis. Even more important, the MVA can take advantage of the experience of TVA, whose engineering aspects have now been largely completed. In the social field, TVA and the new team which builds MVA can learn together—for the problem of adjusting the human being to his environment has now become part of the work of the team.

From TVA's experience it is clear that an ample supply of cheap electric power is, by itself, insufficient to reshape the people as well as the industrial potential. One way in which this is demonstrated in the Tennessee Valley is in the journey which workers are forced to make from their homes to their jobs—sometimes fifty miles each way. The adjustment demanded by nature is total, its aspects many. MVA, if it is to cope with the future, must establish from the first a program for those investors and corporations who will seek to establish industry in that suddenly flowering region. Today, from TVA's experience, it is clear that the size and the location of industrial plants and the residential communities dependent on them must be seen and planned all in one piece, to fit the larger design.

When Congress, responding to the expressed wishes of the majority of the people, writes these objectives into an MVA, we will have made a beginning toward a pattern of vital and decisive political action, essential to democracy's own health. The elected representatives of the people will not do this, however, unless the leaders of those groups of individuals of the country who have most to gain from developing the country are themselves clear in their vision. Lacking an over-all concept they will continue to express and demand the expedient piecemeal solutions. They will continue to be frightened—of technology which might take away jobs, of Malthusian bogies which they conceive to threaten the standard of living, of foreigners and their governments, and of the specter of communism, the challenge of which they continue to meet by condemnation instead of showing, by competition, how democracy does the job better. This lack of faith and this reliance on negatives does not lead to better representative government but to more and more concentration on short-term and narrow motives, which hold back the energies of all the people and restrict the vision and the decisive power of vital democratic government.

The cure for the hesitation, the faltering, and the stumbling of representative government will never be found in negation and fear. It lies in a positive affirmation which will see politics as the vehicle for organizing government to assume society's collective responsibilities. But the leaders of those millions who have most to gain from this orientation of the political apparatus must see the future whole before they can see it at all. They will then see that the business of electing a representative is not for the purpose of legalizing an act of special privilege but to carry out a program which will make of that special privilege, if it is worthy, one strand in a great tapestry of human rights and responsibilities.

An over-all strategy is more necessary in the political and economic fields than it is to create a great enterprise such as TVA, for it is the foundation on which the big projects are built. The representatives elected by the people are, in the last analysis, simply the team selected to carry out a plan. No plan, no execution. Given a plan and an over-all concept, the future belongs in the area of democracy.

In the process of reshaping nature, institutions are perforce molded into a form capable of carrying out the greater functions which Man undertakes. Politics and the quality of government is a first arena of this change. Only a representative government can feel the impact of the people at the grassroots level and carry out their wishes. Only a representative government can be an instrument of the whole country, can see the nation and nature whole and act with that knowledge as its guiding spirit.

To reach this pinnacle, representative government must

turn more and more to those millions who have the least power individually but together are the source of all strength. Those millions of individuals will be reshaped as they learn to know what they want, to have faith in their objectives, and build vehicles of opinion with which to make themselves heard and felt. This has been the line of development taken by the Rural Electric Cooperatives. Dirt farmers, banded together to perform the needed job of bringing light and power to the countryside, are now a group of individuals whose wishes and needs are expressed articulately and forcefully. And as representative government feels this new and added importance of the individual in many fields and regions, it will respond by enabling Man to liberate his energies.

The need now is for the over-all plan as it concerns politics. The trade unions in this country are the organizations which represent the largest numbers of individuals who have the vitality and the interests necessary to carry out a political plan in this context. The higher educational groups have failed. In every field but the physical sciences they spend their time in lament and fear. Their bankruptcy is explicit in the generations who have passed through their hands and have emerged without the equipment or the vision to see the world whole. The most powerful of the financial and economic groups have failed. They live in their old-fashioned concepts of waste and profit. They will not discard their custom-built blinders of power and privilege, since they do not dare to look to see where they are in the world. The majority of farmers, labor's strongest potential ally, are still isolated, unable to see the problems of the world in one piece and dominated by farm organizations which represent special privileged interests. The notable and encouraging exception to this rule is the Farmers Union, whose leaders and members—independent owners of family-type farms—are today far in advance of organized labor in promoting the national interest and the international welfare as part and parcel of protecting their own interests. However, the farmers cannot go it alone. Nor should they have to.

Labor has an enormous stake in the conservation and development of our natural resources. During the last several years, lumber prices have outrun, by a billion dollars, the prices of other commodities. These skyrocketing lumber prices are the result of scarcity which has pinched labor first and hardest. Working people, if they have not been entirely priced out of the home market, have found themselves unable to afford the kind of home they want. The misuse of our forests means continued high prices and progressively more expensive homes for which labor pays—to the damage of its real wages—whatever the increase in the pay envelope. Meanwhile ghost towns, cut-over wastelands, and forest fires, products of a hundred-year policy of "cut-and-get-out" destruction of forests, have already affected workers. Fewer job opportunities, smaller supplies of essential materials, and high prices are the consequences of the lack of conservation in forestry.

Labor's economic interest in agriculture conservation is

equally real. When soils are gullied and gutted by erosion, farmers are turned out of their homes to become migratory workers, to their own loss and to the damage of the organized workers of the country. When an irresponsible tenant farming system forces wastage of the soil, food becomes more expensive in the cities. The worker's ability to buy food is tied to a national policy in which respect of the rights of and duties to the land are cardinal.

Labor is now big enough so that, having recognized its basic interest in resources, it can demand a national policy which will stand up for generations. It can demand programs for mineral development, for fuel and energy, for the protection of soils, range, and forests. The integrated development of our river valleys is the key to this policy of conservation even as it is the guarantee of the jobs, recreation, and low-cost power needed by labor. From the workers in the mine, to those who man the transportation systems through to the workers in the plant that make the final finished product, labor is vitally concerned.

In this problem, detail and general pattern flow together and labor must spark the dynamics of realization, a task to which they are no newcomers. As early as Andrew Jackson's day they were in the forefront. But this time the need is not simply to abolish a privately owned Bank of the United States but to revitalize Mankind. Big and pompous though that generalization sounds, it is nevertheless concrete. For look closely at any big plan—it is but the sum of its myriad details. Those details fit into the whole design;

each detail has a relationship to every other adjacent piece and each is essential to the whole. Like a jigsaw puzzle, a big plan is incomplete if every part is not fitted into it. The political plan for modern America will be equally incomplete if all the parts do not fit. And in a big plan, as in a jigsaw puzzle, there is no room at all for pieces which are not designed to fit. The details cannot be programmed unless there is a general plan in which to fit them.

To create an MVA which will include this kind of overall approach to the adjustment of human beings and nature will take concerted action.

The individual in this or any other country cannot, of himself, be a strong voice in making wise public policy. To be heard, the individual must work through his organization. The problem of more food and of better soil and water management, coordinated in the interest of creating better human beings, belongs high on the agenda of every organized group to which masses of individuals belong. The problems come down to the individual. The goals and the aspirations go up from him, through the organizations to which he belongs and through which he becomes articulate, to great undertakings.

CHAPTER XII

A Drop to Drink

A river is more than an amenity; it is a treasure.
CHIEF JUSTICE OLIVER WENDELL HOLMES
in a court decision

Decisions on the political front will not wait forever. America's water resources are being ruined before our eyes. Without adequate water supplies, the nation will quickly go down; every man will feel the impact.

A man can be happy in a well-watered verdant paradise. He will be a sour and scraggly individual if he goes through the process of watching his homeland become a parched and thirsty barren. In the early days of our West many a man was killed in a fight over a waterhole. Today all of the waterholes are in danger and everyone is in the fight to stop, once and for all, the drive for short-haul profit which imperils the life source of all the people.

An official of the State of Colorado has said that "water is more precious than gold, more explosive than dynamite." Because water gives life it must be guarded, conserved, and beneficially used; when water is scarce it must not be wasted or abused; when it is rampant it must be curbed. Where it is defiled it must be cleansed—lest all suffer.

The term "adequate water supply" is personal, important to each individual and essential to all. The individual can find his relationship to an "adequate water supply" in the glass of water which he drinks and in much else which is essential to him.

American waters generally are filthier now than ever before. This menace to water resources is particularly grave in the old settled New England states and in New York and Pennsylvania. These areas have watched western resource developments as more or less interested bystanders. Suddenly they too are in dire need of remedy. Population and industrialization have jumped, while little thought has been given to vital water supplies. The increase in pollution has been staggering. Rectifying past errors is an immense full-time job. A hundred million dollars is, according to the United States Public Health Service, spent each year just to take the poison out of water so it may be drinkable by the people and usable by industry. Around the clock, every day, sanitary engineers and the medical profession maintain their vigil to keep the forces of gastrointestinal disease from getting out of control. The same pollution has brought severe constriction of the nation's recreational resources and opportunities.

Pollution results in a chemical cocktail which is characteristic of the drinking water of many cities. Visitors to Philadelphia always jibe about the malodorous smell of its rivers, and the curious and unappetizing taste of its water. The displeasing aroma and color of Philadelphia's drinking water can be matched by Cincinnati, Louisville,

Pittsburgh, and numbers of other cities, large and small. Sixty-three hundred American communities, with a population of over 50 million people, still dump their disease-laden sewage into our rivers. To the vicious pollution caused by sewage must be added that which comes from industrial wastes which are dumped into rivers. Dumping of waste from industry is unnecessary and obsolete but the old-fashioned men go right on doing it despite the hazards to health and the insults to the nose and eye which result.

Pollution of water supplies is a national scandal—an outrage which modern minds cannot much longer tolerate in a civilized world. One of the worst offenders is the sulphite paper pulping industry. The waste which it discards so callously into our sweet water supply is not waste at all. It contains considerable amounts of sugars. In other countries, not blessed with the same abundance of foods as we, the governments require that these sugars be converted into alcohol and other products. The waste which now pollutes our rivers and destroys our water supply while it offends our sensibilities is a potential source of considerable quantities of yeast for human or animal food.

It is a silly and damaging paradox. We get worked up about the world being on the brink of starvation at the same time that we waste a potential source of foods—and ruin our own water supply. Meanwhile—paradox or not—in all of North America only two sulphite plants make use of this process, which provides food while solving a big part of the pollution problem. In this case, in our country, the foods which we lose are much less important than the water we ruin, for our water supply is both inadequate and maltreated.

The sulphite industry is but a dramatic example of pollution. An American does not have to be very old to talk with nostalgia of the good swimming and fishing on the river near his youthful home. His saga rarely ends with that reminiscence; sadly he goes on to tell how things have changed. Today he cannot permit his young son to bathe in what he describes as stinking and filthy water. To that individual an "adequate water supply" becomes an intimate thing for, deprived of it and given its opposite, pollution, his water supply has become unfit for drinking. The river which so delighted him in his youth has become unsafe for swimming. Fishing is only a nostalgic memory. All of this is extremely personal and involves health, work, and play. Sooner rather than later the individual father must learn that if he and his children are to enjoy life, he must watch over the sources of his water—whether close by or far away.

Waters pay no attention to political boundaries. Pollution control therefore cannot be left to the individual states. It is a federal problem, and in 1948 a federal so-called pollution control law was passed. But the old-fash-ioned men were in on the making of the new law with the result that the proposition of achieving reasonably clean waters was literally sold down the river. The law does not ban pollution, it makes it easier—at a time when all of our water supplies are diminishing.

The level of fresh water under the surface of the earth of our country is steadily going down—in many places as much as five feet per annum; in water-starved Arizona twice as fast. As the water supply diminishes a "creeping paralysis" can and will overtake our economy. We pump the water up faster than the rain water can sink into the ground. Irrigation of farm land and water for industry take most of the supply.

To industry, the water shortage is becoming a basic problem. New locations for industrial plants are no longer selected because cheap electric power is abundant but because an ample water supply is likely to be permanent. Fuel can be transported more cheaply than water, because industry uses much greater quantities of water. The manufacture of a ton of steel requires about a ton of fuel. It requires more than 250 tons of water. In the chemical industry the amount of water required is particularly high. For cellulose nitrate, the ratio is 5000 tons of water to one ton of fuel.

The water level is going down everywhere as uses mount. Since 1935 the consumption of ground water has risen from 10 billion to 25 billion gallons daily. Texas is seriously affected; so is Pennsylvania. Some western irrigated farm land may have to be abandoned, some eastern industrial plants will have to be moved to new locations, particularly in the ever more important chemical industry.

The United States Geologic Survey has indicated that the level of underground water supply under the 180 square mile area of the Los Angeles coastal plain is about 70 feet below sea level. This is causing a seepage of seawater which endangers the fresh water wells of the area. The pollution comes back into the picture, since the Los Angeles situation is aggravated by infiltration of oilfield brine and industrial wastes. Los Angeles is already water hungry and this scarcity may well cripple its future growth.

Using water for irrigation, industry, and drinking does not by itself lead to the destruction of the water. When water is pumped up for irrigation, it returns to the earth. Irrigation takes place in regions with slight annual rainfall, where the atmosphere is dry. Some of the irrigation water is evaporated and lost to the area but not to the world. It is carried to distant points where it falls as rain. More evaporation is induced by the very vegetation which is being grown. Some water is consumed by the vegetation itself. But the water that penetrates the earth may seep downward to the water table at a very much lower rate than the rate of withdrawal; or it may percolate to some distant reservoir.

The water discharged from industrial plants is frequently polluted, and cannot always be returned directly to its source. Most of industrial water is used for cooling, and a substantial proportion of it is lost to the area by evaporation. In neither case is the water returned to the earth below.

Heavy use of water therefore accomplishes a redistribution of the water supply rather than a destruction of it. But it goes from the spot where it is needed to another spot, where there may be already a surplus, or to the oceans. Until the supply of underground water is brought into equilibrium, all Americans should be pessimistic about any substantial future.

To the resident of New York or Baltimore, what happens to the water supply in California may seem to have no significance, but that is an illusion, dispelled—if you please—on his own dinner table. The direct source of most California water is underground. Year by year that underground water table continues to fall to dangerous levels. Some irrigation wells have already gone dry, some draw only salt water, ruinous to the soil. In many other places the fall in the water table is so great that the cost of pumping the water has become prohibitive. To blame the old-fashioned men for this state of affairs, which at first glance seems to be what the insurance policies call "an act of God," might seem to be carping. Nevertheless the rapidly sinking store of underground water in the Great Central Valley of California—which next to the Nile is the richest valley in the world—is largely the result of the political and economic moves of the giant privately owned utilities and the feudal landowners who operate huge factory farms in California.

The big California commercial farmers, whooping their tribal cry of "individual rights," crowd out every vestige

of individual rights for the smaller farmers. Their processes are inclusive. They use fair means or foul—anything
which will permit them to hog the land and use all the
water. To accomplish both these ends they drive the small
farmers out of the Valley. They disregard the human—
and in many cases legal—rights to the water of their
neighbors, though their rights are as good as those of the
big operators. A feudally minded operator—and there are
many such in the Central Valley—sinks a 200-foot power-
driven well. That well sucks away the life-giving water
that has nurtured the fields of cotton and potatoes and
grapes owned by his neighbors, parching the lands of the
small farmers even as the feudal baron, 1950 style, tanta-
lizingly and cynically exposes before their heartsick gaze
his own water-filled trenches devoted to rice, which consumes more water than any of the other Valley crops but
which is by far the most profitable of the money crops.

  The big California operators despoil their small neighbors' lands the better to acquire them. They sometimes use
the legal pretext of ancient Spanish law and many times
they bother with no law at all. Meanwhile, in their palatial
manor houses, the feudal lords meet together and conspire
to fight the 160-acre limitation which was written into the
Reclamation Law under Theodore Roosevelt.

  The 160-acre law was designed to protect lands, for
which the government supplies irrigation water, from spec-
ulators and from predatory feudal operations of this very
type. Its ideal was to promote an increasing number of

family farm holdings, but the California feudal barons are stronger, as yet, than the will to enforce this law. Up to this minute the government, and particularly the Bureau of Reclamation, has not enforced the 160-acre limitation on the barons of California, and up to this minute small farmers are still being wiped out, their precious lands fitted into the holdings of the large owners and the operating corporations. The great factory farms now extend unbroken, mile on mile. The wide fields owned by the feudal barons are scarred only by an occasional row of tumble-down shacks occupied by itinerant workers, for whose welfare the big landowners have far less regard than they have for their tractors which they maintain so carefully. The obvious result is that the feudal millionaires increase their riches and prove the most cynical of maxims —"them as has gits." The less obvious result is that the land dries out and the water level constantly drops.

Obstructing the enforcement of the 160-acre limitation is only one arrow in the quiver of the feudal California barons. They have been equally successful in stymying the equitable distribution of waters impounded by the government-built Shasta Dam, which could make up to the Valley a part of its steady loss in the underground water. On this front, the factory farm operators work in closest intimacy with the utility giants who have a stake of their own—to usurp for themselves the exclusive right to sell federally developed power.

"Adequate water supply" is personal though complex.

Its implications reach from the home of the family farm in the Great Central Valley of California to the Wall Street offices of utility giants. Entangled are the California State Legislature, the Department of the Interior in Washington, and the men you elected to the Congress of the United States. And in the web too are you—for if the underground store of water does give out in California's Central Valley, you will know it quickly and see its effect soon. California supplies an important part of the fruits and vegetables on your table, fresh and canned.

In Philadelphia, in California, and in all the country between, everywhere and everyone is involved. So critical is the situation that Senator Joseph O'Mahoney is pressing for the appropriation of more than $50 million to develop practicable means of producing usable water from the oceans and from the clouds. Louis Bromfield reports that in Ohio, his home state, where the underground water stores seemed—only a short while ago—to be inexhaustible, certain communities have not sufficient water for the needs of even one additional family. The diminishing water has already signaled the end of expanding industry. Two huge firms, Procter & Gamble and the Youngstown Sheet & Tube Company, cannot build new facilities in Ohio because of the shortage of water needed for industrial purposes. In Baltimore the water table has fallen 146 feet since 1905. Big industries can no longer choose to locate in New York City, where a combination of pollution and lack of reservoir planning has caused a crisis.

If ever there was evidence that Man can destroy the things he values most—because of his shortsightedness—it is in the story of the pollution of the rivers and the mistreatment of the water supply. The underground water supply is the stored rain. And when that storage is exhausted withered crops, dust storms, erosion, thirsty animals and people are part of the result of not having adjusted to nature. It is high time we had an "adequate water supply," conceived in a pattern with every factor of life considered in the whole.

Seen this way the segments of the job, beginning with a badly needed national inventory of water resources and going on to projects such as MVA—which can provide an adequate water supply both underground and above ground for a great region—cannot be considered humdrum so-called public works projects, planned by bookish individuals who think nothing of increasing your taxes. Nor are the parts of the big job simply bonanzas for contractors whose huge creations—dams and power stations—awe the spectator but are entirely without relationship to him.

Water and watersheds are personal problems, machinery such as MVA for protecting them is personal business. Billions of tons of topsoil are lost yearly down the nation's waterways, 750,000 tons down the Mississippi alone, to be deposited as mud flats, steaming in the summer sun, in the Gulf of Mexico.

To the waterway engineer the dirt-colored flow down

the Mississippi has one meaning; to the sanitarian of a city water supply department it has another. To all of us, as people, its meaning is greatest—and most tragic. Flowing past St. Louis and Natchez and New Orleans are wheat from Kansas, corn from Iowa, milk and cheese from Wisconsin, beef and mutton from the mountain grazing states. Homes and education for youngsters go down that turgid river. Play drifts away too, as fish in the streams and ponds disappear, and song birds, rabbits, squirrels, deer, and elk are decimated. The river carries all away.

We can go on fooling ourselves. We cannot fool nature. Man has tried that in many areas. He has ignored the sources of his water and he has been careless of soil, destructive of farms and vegetation—and ruthless toward wild life. The result of fooling ourselves in all these ways has, in many areas, been that Man has been expelled by the deserts which he created himself. Presently we are on the verge of fooling ourselves about the air we breathe. Dr. Louis McCabe, Chief of the Bureau of Mines, Office of Air and Stream Pollution Prevention Research, spoke sharply recently of an extensive "folklore" about smog. He blamed official mismanagement and selfish industrialists—the old-fashioned men again—for delaying and preventing the air pollution control because it costs too much. Meanwhile dangers have piled up to the point where the Surgeon General of the United States, in his 1950 report, cities as a major cause of the nation's ill health the fact that "cities and industries produce enormous quantities of waste that pollute the air, the streams and rivers."

Water, soil, forests, pastures—even the air we breathe —form a complex interacting web. They must be kept in balance or nature retaliates. Experience and technology show the way to utilize nature's beneficent values. Through knowledge of water resources, through the balancing of its uses, through the establishment of the equilibrium of geography and of politics, and through continuing research everyone can personally benefit. The actions of private individuals and even of single regions cannot be unilateral. That is the old way, perpetuating conflicting claims, delaying and obstructing beneficial developments. Balance is the goal.

CHAPTER XIII

Long Steps to a Great Goal

For individual or nation, water is the great essential around which revolves the life on the land. TVA's epochal significance was in the fact that it marked the first effort of a nation to bring and hold in balance water resources and land—to the benefit of the people. It is because they have sensed the importance of this that men and women across the world believe in TVA and that nations everywhere are seeking solutions along similar lines.

In Brazil, on the thinly populated San Francisco River, is one of the greatest hydroelectric power sites in the world. The Brazilian people, recognizing what the development of that great potential resource would mean for their future, have done an unprecedented thing. They have written into their recently adopted constitution a provision for a San Francisco Valley Authority and, to insure its realization, they have set aside—in that same basic document—a fixed percentage of the nation's total revenue. Brazil's action marks the first time in history that a nation has written such a project into its articles of government. It will not be the last, particularly in the light of the emergence of the Asiatic peoples into national freedom and their eager assumption of the responsibility for quick development of great resources for the benefit of their huge populations.

This is already being spelled out in India where plans for The Damodar Valley Corporation are well under way, directed by Indian engineers—with the significant participation of a TVA alumnus. Prime Minister Nehru, on visiting TVA in 1949, said, "In our country TVA is already a legend." The Indian leadership sees the Damodar project not only as the first of many regional developments but as the training school which will equip their people for all levels of operation—and, going far beyond technical phases, will teach the rising Indians the psychological, anthropological, sociological, and cultural features involved in the recreation of the floor of life.

Morris L. Cooke describes the goal of the Indian leadership: "The projected multipurpose treatment of the river and its watershed for forestry, agriculture, fish culture, irrigation, drainage, industrial and domestic water supply, navigation, flood control, power and industry will act as a beacon—showing just how the objectives can be attained and whether the development can be made profitable in the widest sense."

The Damodar project is evidence that India, a great and advanced nation when the present United States was inhabited by a scant population of wandering tribes, is again assuming its rightful place in the world, returning this time—foreign subjugation thrown off—with the point of view, the tools, and the equipment necessary to create a modern environment and culture in which a prosperous people can dwell in peace. And as the Indians themselves see it, the first step—taken now in the Damodar—is to give Indians, by demonstration, confidence in their own capacity. The demonstration will not be lost on the rest of Asia.

The great imperial powers are, as yet, little moved. They fail to hear what India is saying in its Damodar experiment. The colonial powers take the short view and national self-determination is not part of that myopia. But even the short view tells them that the plight of the peoples whom they rule demands alleviation, if they are to continue to rule. The French, in West Africa, have erected a large diversion dam on the upper Niger River, 700 miles inland from the Atlantic Ocean; but even this useful project is tangled in the maze of imperialist contention. The British berate the French, charging them with having taken the water—needed for their project—without a by-your-leave from the British authorities of the neighboring colony.

No doubt the Africans, though appreciative of the constructive attention being given them by their masters, have their own opinions on what all this means—opinions perhaps gleaned in part from the grapevine which tells them it is an Indian, Pandit Nehru, who, as leader of his people, is sparking the Damodar project. They may have heard that it is the Indian conception of what will be beneficial for the Indian people which governs Nehru—not a British or a French edict which decides all.

Whatever antiquated notions she persists in perpetuating in her relationships with the rest of the world, Great Britain, in the midst of a coal shortage, has come to think in more modern terms about her internal situation. Work has begun on the great Loch Sloy Dam in the wild mountains of Scotland. This will result in a hydro project which will increase Great Britain's supply of electricity by one-seventh. For generations Scotland, like all underdeveloped regions, has lost the best of its youth to other more prosperous areas. Now, with electric power in prospect, they will begin to dream of reversing this trend, of keeping their children at home because of greater opportunities. To this end the Scottish people are intensively exploring the possibilities of developing their unutilized or deteriorated resources, of improving their forestry and agriculture, and in other ways—including the use of phosphates—emulating, as so much of the world does, the pioneer achievements of TVA.

What TVA started rolls in ever increasing momentum over all the continents. In Australia's highest mountains, the people from "down-under" are embarked on a project of switching turbulent rivers around, burrowing enormous tunnels, and erecting power stations. Proudly, they call their big job, "TVA's Powerful Pacific Twin." Close to home in Mexico, TVA has made one of its deepest impressions. President Aleman has translated the lesson of TVA into a government department, the Ministry of Hydroelectric Resources, responsible for over-all development measures. First on the Mexican action list is the development of the basin of the river with the beautiful and onomatopeic name of Papaloapan. Here, in the belt of tropical rainfall, is a region of 45,000 square kilometers on which live 200,000 people, which is to have a project similar to TVA, concentrating on erosion control, water storage, and power generation at the head of the river, and on drainage and better navigation below.

Nations far and near have enrolled in the TVA movement. Obviously, we in the United States could do with more of its benefits in other parts of our own country—especially where it would do the most good, as in the Missouri Valley—but the old-fashioned minds hold back that most essential development inside our country; even as India, the oldest of the world's nations, and Israel, the newest, adopt the modern approach which we pioneered.

The future development of Israel is pointed up in the program for a Jordan River Authority in Palestine. The proposals, conceived by Walter Lowdermilk, who has devoted a lifetime to the modern conception of remaking the planet, read more interestingly than fiction.

In ancient days, the Palestinian land had supported large numbers of people, but they had cared for the land and conserved the water. Wars and migrations, however, had changed the picture into a vista of neglect and decline. The soil had washed off the slopes into the valley floors and the coastal plains. Out of the resulting swamplands came a plague of malaria which had depopulated the country. In Roman times Palestine had supported 3 million people. By 1880, malaria and misuse had brought that number down to 300,000—one tenth of its original population.

When Lowdermilk first looked at modern Palestine, his impression was of a land deep in damage and waste. Looking more closely he discovered some remarkable things. Using science, persistence, and intelligence, the Jewish agricultural colonies had, in many small areas, restored the productive capacity of the land and the waters. They, on their own, had demonstrated the possibility that this old and venerated part of the world could once again blossom on a scale worthy of its glorious past. Lowdermilk set to work to explore that possibility.

As Lowdermilk roamed into the hallowed hills and down the historic valleys, he evaluated the difficulties and he appraised the potentials. He found a remarkable similarity between this wasted land and his own native lush California. Lowdermilk drew the conclusion that what had been done in southern California to bring water to land was possible in Palestine. He began a quest into how to make that come true. He found a unique set of conditions in the Jordan Valley which promised that, as the program became a reality, several million people would be able to live on a high standard of living where only thousands have lived in squalor before. The standard of living can, what is more, expand indefinitely. The Dead Sea is one of the greatest sources in the world for potassium, bromine, and magnesium. As salt water from the Mediterranean is introduced into that sea, and as the subsequent evaporation of the salt water in the hot furnace of the Dead Sea bottom takes place, the minerals which are extracted, except for magnesium, will be constantly replenished. The result will be something for the fairy tale writers—a mine which refills as the minerals are extracted from it. Fairy tales in more ways than this, since at present prices, chemists have estimated the value of the Dead Sea minerals as something over $1250 trillion.

The minerals and the electric power to work them; the new land and the water to give it life—all are implicit and all are vital; but one overriding reason makes it most exciting. More people will live in this part of the recreated planet than ever before, and they will live better than in the Golden Age. And it won't be an accident or the result of a military conquest.

The men of Israel looked on their deserts and saw well-watered areas. They were not the victims of mirages. They knew—and in this short time have already demonstrated—that, with science and its tools, they could create a Garden of Eden out of shifting sands. The Negeb Desert, in Palestine, will soon once again be a land of milk and honey. It will be created, not by a miracle, a change in the earth's axis, or a shift in rainfall, but by Man's own efforts.

Intelligence, social organization, and science of a high

order are the ingredients of change in the Negeb. As a result of the Israeli quest to turn its barren sands into a green garden, the peoples of all arid regions have new tools and new hopes. Salt water can be turned into sweet water with equipment developed under the direction of Chaim Weizmann, the chemist-President of Israel. Shortly, a New England corporation will market this desalting equipment internationally. The Sahara may bloom as a result. Using the new equipment and the type of social organization developed by the Israelis, the rest of the Middle East may turn from mass poverty and its push to war into a land capable of supporting many more millions.

In the Soviet Union the problem has been less to harness rivers and to halt floods or erosion than to exploit new resources. There the developments have been described by the English authority, J. G. Crowther, as "Incomparably the greatest effort of organization" in the world. It includes not only the reported use of atomic energy for blasting mountains and canals but more authenticated projects for rerouting rivers, controlling drought, and building electric power plants, together with the development of industry to utilize the resources. Encompassing all that vast land, the whole is a strategical plan for combined development of resources never before used.

Across the planet men have become conscious of the particular human talent—first demonstrated on a large scale in TVA—for constructive changing of the natural environment. Men have learned that their actions can have a profoundly beneficial effect on all of nature, and that this ability for change has grown tremendously through the application of scientific knowledge. These factors are equally true anywhere on the earth and around them men are organizing according to their own needs. The forms of their organizations differ because details, affected by such things as minerals, soil, energy, and climate, differ in every region, along with culture, tradition, financial ability, and access to scientific knowledge and skills.

Success in harnessing these interrelated factors has come to us in TVA earlier than it may to other countries, for we are a comparatively new civilization, with fewer deep-rooted customs and practices than are found in lands with more ancient and ingrained traditions and practices. A smaller, poorer country might find it financially impossible to duplicate TVA. In areas of much denser population and long-established civilizations, the disturbance to the cultural structure could be much more serious.

Everywhere, however, fitted into the complex of culture, economic capability, and the needs of the environment, men are striving for social organizational forms by which, tying water to land, they can change the old historical theme.

Use and abuse of resources is a central theme in history. Civilizations have gone down on the barren remnants of once rich resources and new civilizations have come up, propelled by the discovery of new or formerly unused resources. Expansion and war now, as always before, is in very large part sparked by the desire for resources. By our handling of virginal resources and by the repair of wasted and eroded land and water resources, the theme can be changed.

No better way to say that one road to world peace lies along TVA's lines than to repeat the common expression which sets nations down as either "haves" or "have-nots," words which describe the causes of many wars. But the simple words also reveal why wars settle nothing. Victory in war for the "have-nots" makes them "haves" and the losers "have-nots." The latter go right to work to reverse the order once again, as witness Germany in 1914 and 1939. An answer to the problem of "haves" and "have-nots" lies not in politics and the waging of war to keep or take away existing riches but in working with nature to create enough for everybody everywhere.

The perfection of huge varieties of weapons with which to wage war is still the greatest of all industries. The task of fashioning, on an equally large scale, weapons with which to wage peace is still ahead of us. Weapons for peace are those which can be used to protect and perfect the environment. The simple lightning conductor is a fitting symbol of the weapon for peace. It deflects nature's thrusts and conserves Man's creations. The social organization of human beings into teams to reshape whole regions and countries is the large-scale lightning conductor, repairing wasted lands, guiding the development of virginal resources, and creating gardens out of barrens.

The team—whether in India, the Soviet Union, or the United States—which does this job is acting as a lightning conductor, eliminating many of the causes of war. The planetary reshaping team therefore assumes ever greater strategic importance in waging peace.

One great undertaking which bears on this theme is the "Bold New Program" announced by President Truman in his 1949 inaugural speech. The President said,

We must embark on a bold new program for making the benefits of our scientific advances and industrial progress available for the improvement of under-developed areas.

More than half the people of the world are living in conditions approaching misery. Their food is inadequate. They are victims of disease. Their economic life is primitive and stagnant. Their poverty is a handicap and a threat both to them and to more prosperous areas.

The United States is pre-eminent among the nations in the development of industrial and scientific techniques. The material resources which we can afford to use for the assistance of other peoples are limited. But our imponderable resources in technical knowledge are constantly growing and are inexhaustible.

I believe that we should make available to peace-loving peoples the benefits of our store of technical knowledge in order to help them realize their aspirations for a better life.

President Truman also said, "For the first time in history, humanity possesses the knowledge and the skill." It bears repeating, for implicit is the fact that both needs and capacities transcend national borders. To embrace all humanity requires an international vehicle for carrying out the program. That vehicle is the United Nations. If UN were permitted to become the instrument by which the new and better world of abundance can be built, it would quickly gain stature and power, for its emphasis would move from bickering politics to fuller development of resources in which every country has a common interest.

The great powers—the United States, the United Kingdom, and the Union of Socialist Soviet Republics—are not yet ready to sink their political differences into a joint endeavor for world development, but the peoples of the world as a whole, brought together and unified physically by the airplane and the radio, are ready. As dynamic ideas about the rights of Man spread, and as individuals use their organizations to express the desires which grow out of the ideas, the political considerations of the big nations may be forced to give way to the impact of science and technology, which in the last forty years has advanced more than in the previous 2000 years.

To attempt a "bold new program" unilaterally is to limit it, to run the great risk of watching the bold program grow pallid and timid—the captive of the old-fashioned men who, in the face of a surging world-wide push, continue to demand the private right to do public damage. The consequences may well be a new form of imperialism and nationalism, the opposite of those ideas articulated by the President. The job of socially responsible individuals and their organizations is to articulate their own ideas of paths to President Truman's announced goal so that it will be attained without endangering peace or strengthening the old-fashioned men.

CHAPTER XIV

Earth Control and Birth Control

Accuse not Nature! she hath done her part;
Do thou but thine!

JOHN MILTON

HUNGRY people cannot wait on long-range projects, however fruitful and valuable they will prove. Their immediate requirement is food. Hunger and the danger of famine stalk great regions of the world. To move great projects from the drawing board to reality will take decades. Meanwhile, the countries which are producing great food surpluses face a tremendous responsibility. John Boyd Orr's proposal for a "World Food Board" is the first practical plan for assuming these responsibilities. The World Food Board would, through the United Nations, build up a reserve of food which would level out good and bad harvests. By the use of this reserve and by other means it would stabilize prices in the international market at prices fair to producers and consumers.

At the insistence of our own and other great food-producing countries, which fear that a lack of hard currency will penalize them financially, this plan has been shelved. This despite the fact that President Truman's "bold new program" cannot be realized unless we—of all the peoples on earth—prove that we are willing, not alone to give technical assistance and loans in the future, but to help now from our bulging larder while the need is urgent. Instead of serving as a reason for the obstruction of the creation of the World Food Board, our own great surpluses, the product of fortunate weather and new techniques, should give us a great and impelling interest in better distributing the fruits of our soil, to make them the seedbeds for the future of free peoples.

The truth is that the United States already faces the dilemma of abundance with which it does not know how to live. The yields of both wheat and corn are straining the storage capacity of the country. According to Secretary of Agriculture Brannan, "Taxpayers bought [in 1948] one bushel of potatoes for every three produced and got no good out of them." The potato scandal of 1950 shows an even worse situation. A vast new cotton crop is creating an 8 million-bale surplus. In addition to the huge quantity of eggs in storage, 1950 found 175 million gallons of dry milk, 105 million pounds of butter, and 2¼ million pounds of cheese stacked, along with nearly 200 million bushels of wheat, a million bushels of corn, and a great variety of other farm production, in warehouses, unused ships, elevators, and even caves. In all, $3½ billion has been invested —up to the end of 1949—by the government in this huge surplus. The government pays $500,000 each day for storage alone.

These great American surpluses, which, as part of the stores of a World Food Board would find such beneficial use, are the results of the great upsurge in agriculture which has characterized the last few decades. During the war years of 1942 to 1945, inclusive, American farmers produced about 2 billion bushels more corn than would have been possible during four years of World War I. In a single year of World War I, stem rust destroyed about 300 million bushels of wheat in the United States and Canada, but losses were comparatively small during all of World War II. It is estimated that the efficiency of animal production during World War II was 25 per cent higher than in 1919. The use of farm machinery in World War II released enough land previously used for work animals to feed 16 million cattle or 26 million hogs. In 1900 the production of 100 bushels of wheat required 108 hours of man labor, only 47 hours were required in 1940.

Since 1940, crop production per acre has increased by approximately 30 per cent. In the next decade the gains are expected to be even more spectacular, some estimates of the increase going as high as 50 per cent more than now —or five times the expected population increase. The reasons for this tremendous impetus in production are to be found in the intelligent use by American farmers of the results of research and invention. Scientists are learning more about how to maintain the productivity of the soil, Man's greatest single asset. They are breeding new and better kinds of crop plants and domestic animals;

they are learning how better to protect both plants and animals against disease and insect pests; they have helped reduce the destructive effects of winter cold and summer heat on plants that are used for human food or animal feed. Scientists are showing how better to process and preserve what is produced.

Agricultural technology is just coming into its own. Scientists are continually delving deeper into nature's secrets so that they may not only explain and preserve the present but also predict and improve the future. It is on this factor, science, that the predictions are made for great acceleration of production in the near future in this country. Using only the knowledge and techniques already available, the croplands now in cultivation in other parts of the world which produce only a tiny part of their potential can supply greater quantity and better quality of foods and fibers. However, some techniques, especially of prevention, are still in their infancy. In the United States, insects do more than $4 billion damage each year. Rodents are responsible for a loss of 200 million bushels of wheat annually. Both these losses can be cut with the result that there will be more food for human beings.

However, most of the world's lands are cultivated without proper knowledge of the best use to which the acres can be put. Some, which could be stepped up by the use of irrigation, are devoted to limited grazing or scantily yielding cultivation. Other lands are underused for the opposite reason. They are periodically flooded, marshy, or heavily saturated with salt. On other farmlands, though cultivation is more regularly practiced, primitive methods and poorly adapted crops and livestock yield low returns.

These, with disease, infestation, and uncontrolled climatic conditions, cause the loss of vast quantities of food, fibers, and timber which could be devoted to raising human standards. The prevention of waste, were it to go hand in hand with fairly simple and cheap improvements in implements, methods, seed, animals, and storage, would result in more and better food for large areas in the world. And, of course, in areas now devastated by preventable floods, irrigation projects coupled with the development of hydroelectric power would provide gains for both agricultural and industrial production.

Obviously, should the United States, through the United Nations, undertake to lead a world-wide effort to institute these tested practices, the dark cloud of hunger would grow smaller. Hunger could be entirely liquidated and made part of a sad folk memory if, in addition to more intensively using the lands already cultivated, the effort were to include action to utilize some of the billion acres of usable but uncultivated land as well as to use wood for sugar and yeast and the algae of fresh and salt water for various foods—to all of which specialists have pointed.

Possibilities on the land exist for obtaining food and resources, as varied as are the areas in which they may be found. The Amazon, the Soviet Arctic, Alaska, and Africa are beginning to be explored with this in mind by every kind of political and economic group. The Stettinius Plan in Liberia, the integrated developments by ten companies in Iran, the Day and Zimmerman Project in Korea, and Rockefeller's Basic Economy Corporation in Brazil are explorations of this kind developed by conventional capitalism. At the other extreme is the collectivist development of Siberia. In between are projects which range from those of nonprofit groups such as the Institute of International Education to such glamorous undertakings as the utilization of volcanic heat by Iceland. Emerging forms of social organization in underdeveloped countries join with United Nations activities, in the Food and Agriculture Organization and other agencies, as part of the same world-wide push to explore, understand, and utilize in detail those vast sections which have been for so long hazy blobs on maps.

Canada and the U.S.S.R. have led the way in pushing the wheat belt farther north. Far to the south, cultivation is being pushed into the hotter regions. In Queensland, beef is being produced in quantity. Insects, uneven ground, and lack of readily accessible water supplies—the old enemies—still plague the tropics. Modern insecticides, bulldozers, and well-sinking tools can overcome these obstacles at a price which, while high, will in all probability be less in terms of human energy than now is expended to provide any reasonable standard of living in the tropics. The wartime health service inaugurated by the United States to improve the productivity of the men who, in Brazil, gathered rubber from the depths of the forests,

provided proof not only of this but of the immense possibilities of changing the huge dangerous wilderness of
Amazonia into a healthful and habitable homeland.

Desalting of water, which will produce new arable
land and fresh water supplies in deserts such as the Negeb
and the Sahara, will also be high in first costs. But the
returns are already measurable and they are large. In the
Central Valley of California and in the parts of the Negeb
desert so far developed, the fertile farms, transformed
from barren wastes, have proved to be six times more productive than average lands.

Reclamation of deserts plus expanding utilization of
the hot and cold zones combine to make new physical
worlds which can be developed. Meanwhile most of the
world's food supply continues to come from the old
occupied lands. The people of the settled lands with
ancient cultures are difficult to move into new patterns and
greater production. Old customs, habits, and systems of
production and distribution are formidable obstacles. Because of these, most of the world's food supply, 90 per
cent, is consumed at or near the point of production and
only the remaining 10 per cent finds its way into the world
market. The world's population is still overwhelmingly
agricultural. Most farmers—seven of every ten—raise
food only for themselves and their dependents. They sell
nothing. It is this 70 per cent to whom the rest of the
people of the world must look for more food from the old
lands.

This 70 per cent of the earth's population consists

largely of peasantry—illiterate, inefficient in farming practices, and tied to religious habits, taboos, and traditions which make change doubly difficult. The basic solution is in literacy and education, and while techniques in this field are all too slow in emerging, hopeful signs can be seen. The Mexicans have faced into the problem of mass illiteracy by stimulating a feeling of social responsibility in those who already have some education. The person who can already read teaches, as a matter of civic duty, an illiterate to read and write. The Mexicans have also blazed a trail to teach better ways of living to isolated peasant folk. A team of physicians, sanitarians, recreationists, musicians, and educators goes into an area and coaches the inhabitants in the art of living. This approach may hold epochal possibilities in many lands. Add psychological, scientific, and technological talent and equipment to this team. Voluntarily accepted change can, under this type of guidance, produce not only more food but develop human resources while reducing birth and death rates.

The extension of the teamwork pioneered in Mexico points a way which may bring the agricultural revolution to vast regions. The beginning of a world-wide attempt to grapple with this problem may be seen in the plans of the Food and Agriculture Organization to become County Agent to the world, reaching the farmer where he lives with information which, while extremely helpful for the individual farmer, will relate the problem of the farmer and his own country to that of other countries and the world. Introduction by FAO of comparatively small, in-expensive equipment such as hand cultivators, hoes and scythes, hand tools, insecticides, and spray guns, all of which can be made in village shops, will in itself be of immense value. Add to this the rudimentary teaching of new techniques and the FAO will set out on the road to improving the yields and the lot of farmers now at the lowest end of the ladder.

The job, whether approached by FAO in intensive detail or tackled more generally, will not be easy, for successful achievement necessitates changes in deep-rooted religious customs as well as in traditions of farming. Some patterns of behavior, instilled over centuries, obstruct balanced development. All religions are in agreement that the saving of life and the alleviation of suffering are desir-able. With this belief, the sanitarians, the doctors, the hygienists, and most other scientists are in complete accord —as is evidenced so concretely in pasteurization, water purification, elimination of disease, and so many other activities.

But to extend Man's lifespan is not enough. Every human being must simultaneously be acquainted with the facts of the longer life he has been given. More people will be alive at the same time and if births continue at a high rate, human population in the area may well outrun the capacity of the environment to sustain the increased numbers. Methods of birth control which will make it possible for mankind to voluntarily balance its demands with its environment are essential. To maintain that balance, birth control must be taught simultaneously with the introduction of all the other methods by which men live longer and better. Birth control is as much a matter of technology—as indeed it is also of humanitarianism—as the prevention of disease and the decline of mortality. It is, therefore, entitled to an equal place in the sun, regarded as a necessary step in the creation of a balanced world, where human beings living long and prosperously have all the children they want, but only if they want them.

The necessity for birth control has to be spelled out and emphasized not only in the East but in the western world where the notion that birth control is sinful has been promulgated for so long by the Catholic Church that most people—whether Catholic or not—have been unconsciously conditioned by the sectarian propaganda. Without themselves realizing it, many by-pass the issue of providing the education and means for birth control. The refusal to face into the problem is depriving millions of parents the freedom of choice by which they could themselves determine the size of the family they want, making their decision with some knowledge of the resources which will be available for the support of the family they are creating.

The inculcated tradition and the stated policy of the Catholic Church make the necessary teaching of birth control difficult everywhere including Asia, where dangers of overpopulation are so obvious. The recent blast of the Catholic Church against the Allied Occupation Command in Japan for permitting the teaching of the methods of birth control by contraceptive means is a vivid illustration. The Church embarked on this onslaught while admitting the seriousness of the Japanese population problem. The American Military wilted under the attack, yielding to doctrinaire pressure which will, in the long run, create a serious problem for which the Church offers no solution at all.

Further complicating this task of teaching birth control is the opposition of nationalists who see, in large and excessive populations, the potential of great armies. Those born exploiters of Man who desire large surpluses of labor as a likely substitute for slaves also obstruct birth control teaching. Opposition is indeed strong but it does not make the job of institutionalizing birth control less urgent. For without birth control, stable populations will come only from urbanization and industrialization of the underdeveloped areas, and this, while dynamic and important, will not markedly affect primarily agricultural regions. Birth control is part of integrated human development. Regardless of prejudice against it—based on religious ideas, on militarism, or on the desire to expoit—birth control is an essential to public policy if the world is to provide the basis for a vaulting rich culture in every land.

Intelligent public policy must also recognize another fact which no longer can be evaded. The problem of land tenure is already occupying much of the world, but as yet it is not solved anywhere. Land tenure, like other fundamental economic problems, must finally come to be seen as a matter of rights and duties. Private ownership of the land seems to have proved its incompatibility with the social responsibility which possession of a part of the world's heritage entails. At the opposite end of the economic pole, the collective farm system of Russia seems to be exchanging one evil for another by cherishing the land at the expense of the individual. No one can estimate the damage which the unsettled problem of land tenure is causing, particularly in the old settled lands of the world, yet—even within the limitations of backward public policy —changes in the pattern of food production and distribution do occur.

As late as the eighteenth century, England and Denmark were nations of peasant farmers, whose output and practices were on the same low level as that of the present-day peasants of eastern Europe. The British and Danish farm systems have been changed entirely. Farm size is neither tiny nor huge, but suited to the abilities of one man and his helpers. A blend of livestock and arable farming has taken the place of single crops. Once the change was effected, the productivity per acre and per man started to rise and is still rising, bringing with it in Denmark a standard of living and a high efficiency of production which is the envy of all Europe.

The fundamental mark of change from peasant to modern farmer is that the peasant produces only for himself and his family, selling only his surpluses, while the western farmer produces for the market. He is dependent on the market—his products must satisfy the requirements of that market, which means he cannot live in isolation. If he is not familiar with techniques, if he does not learn to care for his soil, if he pays no attention to breeding or to yields, his produce will be inferior to that of his competitors. His production—if inefficient—will be more expensive. The pattern of his farming requires that he be educated and that he cooperate with others. Both education and cooperation enhance his ability cumulatively. In the process, each farmer's value as a husbandman becomes greater. Were just the latter achieved on a universal scale we would have fewer worries about soil exhaustion. Soil never fails; the husbandman fails. Wherever the husbandman is dynamic, moving forward, the soils are and will be more fertile than before.

Because farming has in large part changed from peasantry to growing for a market—and, of course, because of the impact of science—the food supply in the western world is in no immediate danger. In more than half the countries of the world containing at least 40 per cent of the people, the production and the quality of food have been continually improving. In those countries the output of farmers has increased, the rate of population growth has slowed down, and diets for all have become better. These are the first results to come from the improvement in the pattern of farming, increased use of technology and mechanization, and the increase of education.

This situation has not been paralleled in the East because the Orient has not yet had the benefits of modern science and technology. Every effort expended to bring the East up to the western scientific and technological and industrial practices and standards will, on the basis of the West's record, mean that in the next half century the East and West could live in a single peaceful world, neither overpopulated nor poverty-stricken.

The technical knowledge and skills which have already been developed in the United States would, if applied fully, result in a new agricultural revolution in most of the world. The nineteenth century is known as the century of the industrial revolution; the second half of the twentieth century could complete the agricultural revolution. In the operation of fully mechanizing the productive processes, the nature of farm labor itself will change, so that the unskilled farm hand will tend to become more like his skilled city counterpart. The age-old differences between agricultural and industrial work are already being destroyed by machinery, common to both. As agriculture takes on the variety of industrial production the gap between city worker and farmer will close.

The last half century has seen the emergence of agriculture as the country's largest industry embracing—for production—ever increasing industrial sources of supply such as fuel and power, machinery and chemical fertilizers, and at the other end of its cycle—consumption—an industrial capacity which utilizes a growing share of agricultural production in the making of products for medicine, structural materials, synthetics, and chemicals. In our time all these have become branches of agriculture as an industry, and this development will grow as the agricultural revolution proceeds. Meanwhile the ancient agricultural ideal of self-sufficiency for each farmer moves to an interdependency which is world-wide. All this is a revolution that does not maim or kill but helps maintain life. It is a revolution which makes it possible for the world to feed and clothe itself more easily and surely than formerly.

From the elimination of taboos to the completion of the agricultural revolution with its abundance involves a set of steps which are intensely practical. As yet we take those steps stumblingly, both in earth control and birth control. What we do is piecemeal, almost never related to all other factors which, if taken together, would result in a higher standard of living, obviating the economic advantage of or even the necessity for a large family. The era of the biological necessity that many children be born so that a few might live is receding into history. As amply demonstrated in the richest countries, the way to reduce a surplus of people is to create a surplus of food.

CHAPTER XV

Universal Resources

THE speed with which the world's standard of living will go up or down is tied as much to fuel as it is to food. In fact, the amount of food which can be grown is determined by the amount of fuel which is available for the making of tools, machinery, fertilizers, insecticides, and a great variety of other necessities. Fuel is the foundation on which our civilization is built. Reduce its supply and you reduce the amount of steel which can be manufactured—and of clothing, drugs, and everything else. Reduce the amount of fuel, commercially available, to zero—and our way of living would disappear into unheated mud and log huts. In full circle horses and oxen would again supplant trains, planes, and automobiles. Communication networks would extend no farther than the sound of a drum, beating out a message.

The picture will never be as dark as that, but since our dependence on fuel in large amounts is so obviously total, shortages can be critical. As our own industrial capacity grows, and as the rest of the world industrializes and mechanizes its agriculture, we head into expanded use of every fuel on which we are now most dependent. By far the largest portion of the world's people is engaged in agriculture, which even in the United States is only partially mechanized. Two million American farms still need electric power; farmers walk eight or ten miles daily to do work which could be done by pushing a button. Electricity, tractors, trucks, and automobiles all require fuel. Where will it come from? At present, of course, the largest portion of electric power comes from fuels such as coal and oil. Oil is the great requirement for internal combustion engines. But despite the best efforts at conservation it is too easy to read the handwriting on the wall. Mineral fuels—most particularly oil and gas—will one day be scarce and therefore so high in cost that they cannot be used economically. That day comes closer as electric power is more widely used—as it should be and must be. The time has come to look up, down, and around for energy sources, to find new supplies and to program their development and use.

Waterfalls already supply a small percentage of the need for electric energy. The expansion of hydro power to its outermost limits is urgent. Canada already uses water power for about 98 per cent of its electricity. The United States, though rapidly increasing its hydroelectric generation, can develop much more in the Missouri Valley and other regions. Africa has the largest potential hydroelectric production in the world, about four times as much as North

America, but it does the least with it, producing now about one per cent of the amount generated in North America. Africa does not lack rich resources. Its great need is for the evolutions of forms of social organization which will efficiently use those resources. However, hydro—were it to be developed everywhere—has not the potential necessary to produce more than a fraction of the total electric power required by the world.

For the greatest and constant source—naturally and inevitably—we will look to the sun, prime source of energy. Our little planet receives only one two-billionth of the sun's energy, but this tiny fraction is tremendous, its value calculated by Eugene Ayres in his great paper, *Major Sources of Energy*, to be worth, at current rates, about $2 billion a minute.

Solar radiation is most intense in the world's arid regions, an area of the world's surface considerably larger than the total fertile area. Over these arid areas a large proportion of the solar radiation is not fixed by vegetation. It is absorbed in the day and lost in the night. If this mighty loss could be avoided, the world could utilize this vast amount of solar energy. This can be done once we succeed in duplicating the ability of plants to capture energy from the sun's rays. Chlorophyll, the green coloring matter, does the jobs for plants. The extremely rapid progress in chemical research, using radioactive carbon and other isotopes, encourages scientists to believe that Man can one day synthesize chlorophyll and with it secure energy directly from the sun's radiation. The substances called semiconductors—already used in some photoelectric cells—also convert the sun's radiation into electric current. Direct application of chlorophyll and these semiconductors may yet make the great deserts in Africa and Asia, Australia and America the main centers of world energy production. In the United States the Massachusetts Institute of Technology is pursuing an intensive program in this work, its research in photochemistry, photoelectricity, and thermoelectricity aimed at the target of utilizing the sun's radiation.

In this period when industrialization is still restricted to small areas, most of the energy required all over the world is for the provision of warmth. Direct solar radiation can answer this need in a period much shorter than that required for solving the problem of using solar radiation for the making of electricity. Flat collectors of the sun's heat—operating on the same principle as greenhouses—are being intensively researched in several United States universities. Such a heat collector, made of the most modern glass, attains very high interior temperatures. Even now it is easy to keep a house designed to use a heat collector comfortably warm, even in mid-winter, as long as the sun is shining and without burning any fuel at all. But always the problem in solar house heating, as in solar power production, is to store the heat while the sun is shining so that it can be used during the night and during long protracted overcast skies.

Usually water heated during the day is used for this purpose. In Switzerland a water-storage system, sufficient to bridge over ten or twelve sunless days, has had a long test period. Even during the wet summer of 1946 it was found that the water could be heated to the boiling point. An average house requires only about 15 cu. ft. of water as its heat storage reservoir. At M.I.T., a solid, Glauber's Salt—a cheap chemical—is in use. It is capable of storing at least seven times as much heat as water.

Use of solar radiation for home and hot water heating is far beyond the speculative stage. If you live south of a line which passes through Philadelphia, Chicago, and San Francisco, a house can now be designed for you which will consume practically no fuel. While solar-heated houses still cost more to build than do conventional houses, the added initial cost is, because of rising fuel costs, already almost justified on the basis of heating alone—and solar-heated houses have the added advantage of being air-conditioned in the summer.

The usefulness of solar-heated houses is not limited to the latitudes south of Philadelphia. Houses in New England can be built to eliminate 85 per cent of the fuel. Architects and engineers have progressed so far with their work in solar heating that widespread installations are a reasonable expectation. You can already purchase a solar-energy collector on the open market. Though somewhat primitive as yet, prefabricated houses designed for solar heating are offered now, but the efficiency will skyrocket as the cost of fuels soars. House heating is more than a third of America's total energy requirement. As the utilization of solar energy goes up, wood and mineral fuels are conserved.

These are the great broad applications of direct solar radiation. So important do they now become that the Secretary of the Interior is considering asking Congress for funds with which to conduct large-scale research to hurry the utilization of solar energy. Another but narrower utilization of the sun's warmth is the heat pump, a contrivance which collects heat at a certain temperature from the earth, a body of water, or the air and delivers it at a higher temperature to a home or any other building. To raise the temperature, a gas is compressed when it is returned after circulating through coils in contact with the heat source. This apparatus is identical to the ordinary household refrigerator and can, in fact, be reversed for summer cooling. The additional energy, of course, is derived from the sun. The heat pump is increasingly important as we become more dependent upon electric energy rather than upon fuel combustion. The electricity which powers the pump requires fuel—as heat collectors do not —but heat pump fuel savings are very large.

The heat pump produces only the low potential energy suitable for space heating. A higher potential energy suitable to generate electricity can be garnered by utilizing the differences in temperature in the tropics between the ocean surface and its depths. It is conceivable that the shorelines of tropical seas could some day be the sites of power plants which would rival our present hydroelectric installations. Along these shores the surface water temperature often exceeds 90 degrees, warmer by over 40 degrees than the sea water 1500 feet below. This difference is sufficient to operate a vacuum steam turbine. In 1930, Georges Claude, the French inventor of the neon gas tube for electric lighting, devised a long pipe line which he tried to anchor in the sea. He failed in that try but the French government is currently backing a similar venture on the Ivory Coast in French Africa.

The earth radiates energy—more even than it receives from the sun. Little of the great heat of the earth's interior can as yet be used. The one exception is volcanic steam. In Tuscany stands the world's largest power plant of this type, turning out a steady supply of electric energy. Italian scientists are suggesting burrowing a tunnel into Vesuvius as a possible end to Italy's everlasting need for coal import. Vents of volcanic steam exist in many countries, but even in the aggregate they are not consequential. A small power plant at Geyser, California, is the only volcanic steam utilization in this country.

Tidal power is still another of the constant energy sources. Were all the tidal energy harnessed, it would amount to about one-half of our present power requirement. However, as a practical matter, there are only a dozen points in the world where tides are of sufficient magnitude to justify installations. The mouth of the Severn

River in the British Isles is one of these spots. Others are the Passamaquoddy, in Maine, which with its neighbor, the Bay of Fundy in Canada, comes back into the news frequently. All three of these tidal sites would, if developed, furnish only a minute percentage of our total yearly requirement.

The only great sources of energy, among all these possibilities, are solar radiation, water power, and the heat of the earth. The heat of the earth, except for volcanic power, cannot yet be utilized on any wide scale. The amount of water power that can be obtained is forseeable. It is important, but it will not be sufficient. This leaves only solar radiation as the great source of continuous energy.

What then of atomic fission as a source of power? Most people look with great hope to the harnessing of atomic energy as a source of practically inexhaustible power. Only two heavy elements, uranium and thorium, continually undergo atomic transformation and generate heat. The secret which the scientists learned about these minerals is how to accelerate the process which goes on naturally at all times. Great acceleration creates an atomic-bomb explosion. Moderate acceleration provides a possible source of power. The rate of acceleration can be regulated and it is being done successfully in the graphite piles. The temperatures produced in the pile can be made correct for the generation of steam, and an experimental plant to create electric power is promised before the end of 1951. The cost of uranium-produced power will be only a little more per kilowatt-hour than the cost of fuel, but—and this is the rub—uranium reserves may not last any longer than petroleum reserves.

A reason for pessimism with regard to the prospects for peaceful utilization of atomic energy is the rate at which uranium is being used for bomb manufacture. Although we are not told what this rate is, we can make an educated guess. The annual production of uranium in the world is reported to be more than one thirtieth of the entire known reserve. Even though the rate of production does not increase over the next thirty years, no rich uranium ores will be left. If that line of destructive action continues, atomic fission may be sacrificed by the old-fashioned men on the altar of Mars. Bertrand Russell, in acid comment, summed up the nature of the dilemma. "The supply of uranium in the planet is very limited and it is feared that it may be used up before the human race is exterminated."

This is not to say that atomic energy, turned to peaceful purposes, would not be of profound benefit. If the bomb-makers can be deflected and atomic energy used for peace, poverty-stricken peoples now living in barrens and deserts can achieve a standard of living—using atomic power—comparable to that of the people of nations rich in coal and oil. Great industrial nations, with the help of atomic power, could complete the process of making machine and factory operation more automatic, basically changing conceptions of workbench and work time and the role of men involved in the process of mass production. Atomic energy has, indeed, other possibilities than as the great destroyer.

Whatever the atomic future holds, our chief dependence now is upon the coal, petroleum, and natural gas which were formed millions of years ago by geologic change. Man's intensive use of these fuels began about 100 years ago. More than three quarters of all the coal which has been mined has been taken out of the ground in the last several decades. Petroleum production has been concentrated into even a shorter period. Obviously, one day in the not too distant future, we are going to come to the end of the period when fossil fuels are used on any large scale. The reserves are tiny when compared to the needs— in fact the whole era of the use of fossil fuels can be regarded as very short, and quite the opposite of rich in energy resources. The next era—now on the horizon—will be one of plenty, using ever present, universal, and constant energy sources. We are embarking now on the transition to the newer era and to effect it requires planning and much work. A start toward the new systems of energy production and consumption is immediately necessary; and, as this work goes on, every effort to retard the wasting of coal and oil and gas and to conserve their supplies must be made. The creation of synthetic liquid fuels is, of course, also an essential toward meeting the presently expanding needs.

The trend toward utilization of universally available resources such as solar radiation goes far beyond fuels and sources of energy. Sixty per cent of the mammoth DuPont Company's sales are in products that did not exist or were not being made on a commercial scale as recently as 1926.

By far the greatest part of these products is raw materials used by other companies in making finished products. DuPont's laboratories and factories have become colossal mines and croplands, supplying raw materials—metals, fibers, and resins—which formerly were taken out of the ground or grown on the land.

The DuPont pattern can be duplicated over the entire world. Limited local resources such as copper and rubber are being supplanted by universally available resources which, with the aid of science and industry, can be obtained almost anywhere in any desired amount.

The trend of supplanting local resources with perpetually and universally available substitutions began about fifty years ago. Then the big fear was that the world supply of nitrates would shortly be exhausted. Scientists were acutely conscious of the fact that, once the nitrate supply was gone, fertility of the soil everywhere would suffer from lack of fertilizer. Today the world has an inexhaustible supply—taken from the air. The air is as much a mine as are the Chilean nitrate fields, and nitrates from air are available everywhere in the world where industrial facilities are erected. Over each square mile there are 20 million tons of nitrogen in the atmosphere.

That was the beginning of many developments in which human resourcefulness became a major ingredient in resources. The list is now long. Nylon has already displaced silk and is becoming an ever more familiar substitute for cotton fibers. Its sister product, orlon, is about to come into use in place of wool. Made from material we have always called waste—the chaff from wheat, corncobs, oat hulls, and the stalks of sugar cane—plastics in a thousand forms do the work of wood and light metals. Synthetic rubber is already more efficient than natural rubber in many ways, and it may soon be cheaper. Jute is being replaced by a synthetic, and cocoanut oil is giving way to a factory-made product. Atabrine serves instead of quinine.

Meanwhile the trend has pushed toward greater use of substances which can be found everywhere. Common clay and other basic materials have become aluminum—which does not exist in nature. Aluminum is a man-made metal which takes the pressure off the need for rarer ores. The utilization of the magnesium in sea water is still another prime example of the new tendency. Every cubic mile of ocean contains six million tons of magnesium and the oceans' 300 million cubic miles will not soon be exhausted. Potassium is still another. All this is a good deal more important as a factor in the pattern of the world's resources than as a demonstration of how clever and ingenious we human beings are. In fact the emerging pattern is on the way to becoming the brightest prospect not only for the survival of the race, but for the creation of abundance. The resources on which we have depended are localized—iron or oil fenced in by nations—breeding war. The substitutes now being found are available internationally, making possible the realization of the dream of free access to resources by all nations.

We live on the "line of discovery" in this little-noticed trend toward universal solutions for resource needs. We cannot guess its boundaries. Foods and drugs are among the latest to feel the impress of the drive toward universal solutions. Lowly molds, nurtured in laboratories, have already become penicillin and streptomycin. Vitamins can and are being produced almost everywhere. Cattle, fattened by urea, will soon be eating a food made from air. In Canada, manufacturers are demanding that the government let them produce coats made of nylon fur because they are warmer than furs made of animal skins.

The trapper on his lines in the northern snows may not have yet heard of nylon fur. The Hindu grower of jute and the great cotton, rubber, and quinine planters, and all the millions who live on the plantations, may not have yet heard of the developments in their fields. But all these and many others will be affected.

Some, like the Japanese cultivator of silk worms, have already felt the impact of science and industry as a natural resource. Our cotton growers can testify to the drastic consequences of nylon and rayon. The Fats and Oils Section of the Department of Agriculture has felt the dislocation brought by the development of synthetic detergents. It is clear that the road from the old world of limited resources to the new world of universal supplies will indeed be rough unless, along with these great strides toward perpetual plenty, the shock is cushioned. Great Asiatic areas, subject now to recurring famine, can raise on these rich plantation lands—no longer needed for fibers or rubber—ample food for all their millions. The transition to plenty demands plans and planning to avert the disasters of dislocation.

Meanwhile the march toward universal resources continues. On every front these are coming from scientific participation in nature's production—accelerating it where more of an element is needed, decreasing or diverting it where it is harmful. And each path leads to a solution which insures an unending supply, universally available. Though the evidence is not yet conclusive, it may well be that we are leaving an era when we needed to explore, find, mine, and exhaust the supply of a material. If the trend accelerates it will be the laboratories and factories which will supply all the strategic raw materials for which Man now scurries over the earth—warring for possession of that which is destined to disappear in use.

CHAPTER XVI

The New Geologic Force

Great things are done when men and mountains meet;
This is not done by jostling in the street.

WILLIAM BLAKE

THE pattern which emerges from an examination of the trends toward the creation of universal and perpetual supplies of resources, the reshaping of whole regions, and the transmutation of deserts into gardens is, in the eyes of some scientists, of tremendous significance. The great Russian scientist, V. I. Vernadsky, looking deeply into the record of human activities has affirmed that instead of making a final exit from the stage of history, as the prophets of doom contend, Mankind is making a grand entrance into a new age. Man, on the basis of all the evidence, is—as Vernadsky has stated it—becoming a great geologic force, capable of reshaping the planet. This is happening not as the result of a conscious act of will, but as the latest culmination of the natural evolutionary process.

This new stage in the history of our planet, the evolution of Man into a great geologic force, has been in the making over a long period. Even before 1859, when Darwin published his pioneering work on evolution, a great American geologist, Joseph LeConte, spoke of the "psychozoic era," which in a sense embodies the same concept of Man's ascendant powers. In France in the eighteenth century, Buffon, prophetically observing Man's impact on the earth, predicted "The Realm of Man."

To understand the reasons for Man's growing power a young American scientific contemporary of Darwin's, J. D. Dana, undertook a long and fascinating quest. As a result of his studies he concluded that over the course of geologic time—at least two billion years—an irregular process of growth and a perfection of the central nervous system has occurred. Dana found that this, while true of all the animal kingdom, had special meaning for Man. His conclusion was that the brain, once it achieves a certain level in the process of evolution, will never go backwards and must move ever forward.

With the beginning of the twentieth century, the human brain's development had progressed so far that Man was brought into a new and startling relationship with nature. It is less than fifty years ago that Man began to demonstrate consistently his ability to change that realm in nature where life can exist—the biosphere. This is a fairly restricted zone of our planet, and it consists of a thin layer of earth less than two miles deep, the oceans, and the lower areas of the atmosphere. In this zone the temperature is about the same as that at which water remains a liquid and all of it is accessible to radiation from the sun. All living matter is concentrated into this small part of our planet.

Man has always shown a tendency to change this zone, but his ability to alter or extend it in any consequential way has been minute until now, when he begins to push with great surges into the future, his progress accelerated and his confidence heightened by his achievements of the past.

We have the benefit of all our yesterdays. Through the centuries, the flakes of knowledge have rolled into a gigantic ball to which each new fact and each new discovery have added weight and size. The ball of knowledge is huge now and it makes all the jobs ahead easier.

The accumulation of this great body of knowledge, coupled with the growth of the power of the nervous system and the mind, has brought results. Look at the record of inventions, the prime field of human ingenuity and resourcefulness. As one invention leads into another the desired effects are not only better each time, the new discoveries are thousands of times more effective. The flail and the cradle were early agricultural inventions. With their help a man laboriously reaped and threshed a bushel of grain in forty hours. The modern offspring of these first inventions is the self-propelled harvester-thresher, which is only a few years old. Today a man reaps, threshes, and delivers a bushel of grain in less than a minute. A single farmer, using a modern thresher, can produce more wheat now than did whole countries in ancient times.

With the first megaphone a man sent his voice a few

hundred yards farther; but with radio he spans the earth with his voice. The invention of the wheel permitted our forefathers to travel a few more miles each day; but the invention of the airplane increased the radius of travel by thousands of miles.

That same mankind which is said to be doomed has changed the geology of parts of the earth just as effectively as the Ice Age changed the face of the land. When the first settlers came to southern California they found a natural desert, a good climate, and an ideal location. They wanted to stay and they did. Men—and not nature—have changed that desert into a green garden, almost unmatched in the world. Simple irrigation in the ancient style would never have done the job. The meandering San Joaquin River did not have enough water. Into the desert went the scientists and the engineers. They wrote a drastic and logical prescription which could be filled because they had the most modern tools as well as knowledge. They piped and pumped water south from the distant Sacramento River into the desert country. There they released the flow into the San Joaquin River and made that dribbling stream a stable river, far stronger than it had ever been. One half acre in the Valley, barren desert not long ago, now supports a man. Three acres are required in most of the world. Nothing grew here before. Now this land is six times as good as the average.

Everyone accepts this achievement, a desert made into a paradise, but not many know that to make the paradise of Southern California the waters of the Sacramento River have been made to run uphill for many miles to feed the San Joaquin at its source. Without violating the natural water course, both rivers—one with more water than needed, one with less—have been fused into a single new water system which never existed in nature.

The Central Valley of Southern California is only a small part of a big change. Where water is plentiful Man moves it, taking it from an overwet area to one where water is needed. This transfer of water has been achieved on a huge scale in the great Colorado-Big Thompson Trans-Mountain Diversion Project. Water is taken from the headwaters of two turbulent mountain rivers on the west slope of the Rockies and carried through a thirteen-mile tunnel carved out of the heart of the great Rocky Range. It emerges on the dry east slope, supplying irrigation water and hydro power, which together make more food and more industry. Serious consideration is now being given to a much greater project of this kind. A thousand-mile system of tunnels and pipelines, burrowing through a gigantic mountain range, may join the great Columbia River system with that of the Sacramento to provide water for southern California while relieving the swollen Columbia of flood danger.

The shoreline of the oceans, where live the heaviest concentration of the world's population, is a geologic formation on which Man works his alterations to a startling degree. Land fills extend the size of communities. New

York City's lower west side has been greatly augmented over the years. In San Francisco the large and verdant Golden Gate Park was, not so long ago, a deserted windy vista of sand dunes. The ocean and the seas are valuable—indeed the Soviet Union, observing with alarm the drying up of the Black Sea, has diverted several rivers which formerly emptied into the Arctic so that they now replenish the Black Sea. And who does not remember the dramatic creation of artificial ports, towed into Omaha Beach on D-Day, Man's attempt to find a quick answer to unfavorable geology.

The floor of Man's existence, the earth and the water, have already seen, in this and many other countries, geologic change fostered by modern Man. So also has the atmosphere above. Our own creations have completely overturned the old realities of distance and time. The perfection of the airplane and the faster rocket has brought places—remote from each other as the distance is measured in miles—ever closer. The mile that separates is no longer a mile; it is an ever shortening time unit.

Electronically controlled telescopes pull planets and stars nearer to the eye. The great telescope now installed at Palomar doubles the power of the best of its predecessors. Rockets and guided missiles drive farther and farther into the firmament. Before aviation was discovered we went no higher than the tallest mountain. Today rockets have breached 250 miles. As they push out farther, explorations penetrate the mystery of ocean depths, the record dive of 1949 going 4500 feet down. The envelope of life—the biosphere—is being expanded.

Millions of years ago a single geologic era created the basis of most of our coal. Today we make fuels synthetically, tailoring them to meet our needs. The Ice Ages, coming and receding, scoured out our lake and river beds. We create our own lakes and we call them reservoirs. We place our lakes where we need them and diminish or increase the flow of rivers as it suits our purpose, sometimes changing their course so they run in a direction opposite to the natural flow. The Ice Age ground rock into rubble and started the process of making topsoil. Now we use fertilizer, and introduce worms and other living matter to improve soil, and we do it on those spots where we want to plant. It took many geologic eras to evolve races and strains of animals and plants. In our time we have watched Luther Burbank and others develop new races of plants and have seen breeders of animals come up with new strains.

Some areas are arid, others overwet. Dr. Irving Langmuir of General Electric Company has, by using a mechanical apparatus, "modified the planet," bringing rain to dry New Mexico when the chances that a particular rainstorm would be produced by nature were, according to him, 1 in 1,000,000,000,000,000,000,000. If we haven't changed the seasons yet, we have begun to adjust to them. Only a few years ago no one could grow wheat in the frozen North. The season was too short. Today, with perfected seed and scientific soil treatment, wheat not only grows but the crops become larger each year.

This is the record of accomplishment and discovery dealing with the old and familiar physical world. But we have also raised the curtain of a new, a second world. We now make resources and substances which were previously unknown. We release forces that in quality and intensity are not to be found in the natural world.

Long ago there was an age dominated by the dinosaur. But the dinosaur lacked the power of developed intelligence and that is the difference—a difference which meant his extinction. We have lived through the Stone, the Bronze, and Iron Ages. We have entered, as human history is chronicled, the Age of the Mind.

CHAPTER XVII

Mind Over Matter

From one point of view intelligence is the ability to evaluate Man's two great and constant problems: how to come to terms with his kind. The higher the intelligence, the better the evaluation and the greater the chance for survival—and of a happier and more rewarding life.

STUART CHASE

In the material world great expectations are in order. An expanding and rich material world is in sight. We have taken only the first few steps and yet this we already know—that the large mass of mankind which is half-frozen and starving need not long be so. Man can provide energy, raise the temperature, and increase the food supply. He can create, out of common elements, from salt water to the sun's heat, new and ever renewing resources which will win him a lasting surcease from poverty and misery.

But gaining material ground will mean little if mankind at the same time loses moral, ethical, and spiritual ground. The changes can mean much if, as abundance becomes possible, Man's own stature, his quality, increases. A clue as to whether this will be a result may be discovered by what TVA, first of the new type projects, does in the future.

TVA and the social organization which it brought into being are now well along on the project of mending the Valley to which its work has almost entirely, and necessarily, been confined. Now the TVA team is arriving at a new stage. The reclaiming and the repairing job is almost finished. Ahead lies the bigger job of creating new resources—ethical, social, and spiritual requisites for harmony and peace.

Conflict and war cannot be abolished by any single means. Rich resources do not necessarily make a peaceful country, nor are all poverty-stricken nations aggressive. The mind and the emotions are involved, but these also are part of nature. In TVA, study of all these interrelationships is possible. Here remedies can be sought.

The Tennessee Valley can now become the scene of the creation of these positive values—a result of the teamwork to adjust to all nature. That adjustment, in its present early stage, has already brought the Tennessee River under control as part of a larger plan which included improving navigation, building the multiple-purpose dams, and unleashing the electric power in the falling water. These material changes need not remain simply adjustments to physical nature. They can be fully integrated with the needs of the three million people in the Valley. Each segment of the accomplishment has a part in creating a new culture and a new pattern of life.

Not only the land but the farmer will be remade, not only the cities and towns but the workers will be reshaped

—to the benefit of all. The ultimate success of TVA as a form of social organization will come when its work has made it possible not only for human beings to be more prosperous but for them to live more creatively. Changes in the organization of the life of the community are part of this, as they are reflected in the schools and what is taught in them; recreation and the use of leisure time; and concern for the well-being of all the people.

The value of the work of TVA will finally be measured in terms of the culture which evolves. The contributions of the individuals to literature, music, art, and abstract science; the development of constructive social leadership; a desire to cooperate with others; a high quality of citizenship; a growth of knowledge and breadth of vision—all these are factors which must emerge in the years ahead. The future holds a greater challenge in improving human values than has been met so far by the TVA team. Tomorrow's questions in TVA are not around the value of more hydro power, better navigation, flood control. Those answers are well known. The basic question is the worth of these as they affect the pervasive culture of the individuals and the communities in which they live.

Voluntary association, the unique quality of democracy, has taken this first and purely American project of planetary reshaping as far as it now is. Only democratic action could have done it. The measure of the success which TVA has so far achieved and its prospects for final success rest squarely on the support which the human beings involved in it bring to it. The inescapable deduction is full of hope for those peoples who treasure democracy. An authoritarian country might seek to remake the land by decree. Totalitarian pressure will never remake the individual. In TVA, local and community participation is an essential to success, a necessary part of the modern method which weaves into every man's life the spirit for remaking the land and the people.

To realize the future, all the people must be aware of its impacts and its possibilities. Unless they all pull together, neither they nor the TVA team—however good it is—will succeed. The hope of attainment lies in the progress so far recorded. Its essence is in the integrated approach to total adjustment which includes participation and consideration for the democratic spirit and the freeing of individual energies.

The time has come when we must be equipped not only to grapple with the problem of the conservation of material resources but with that of human resources. Just as we have tackled the physical environment and reshaped it in the Tennessee Valley, we can go to work on the problems of human beings in the cities as well as on the land.

Urban dwellers are suffering from great and complicated frustrations of which the failure to understand and bring into adjustment a machine civilization is the most important. Residents of the great cities are emotionally adrift and without roots. Too many individuals have failed to find peace of mind in the shadow of the machine. Defeated and frustrated, they have succumbed to the widespread fear that the metal monsters would soon dominate all living, inevitably wiping out all vestiges of the creative life of the arts and the spirit. Legitimate though these fears have been, these people stopped their quest too soon and they have missed the point.

The release of those forces which stoke the fires of creative living is as implicit in the work that the machine does for mankind as is the monotony of the automatic operations which has ground out so much social havoc. The fault is not in the machine, but in a failure to understand its mechanical effects. When Man first discovered fire he began a long apprenticeship in dealing with what is both useful and dangerous, and the end is not yet. Man's mastery of his techniques has as yet rarely been so great as to permit him to complete the circle back to nature. He invents a machine to do a job. He does not see—cannot understand because he does not know—the complicated effects that machine may have on the entire web of life.

The machine does something to the man who works at it, it has an impact on the society which is shaped by it. Both these effects contain much in them which are bad. Man is conscious of these defects, speaks of them constantly, and alarms himself by thinking where they can lead. Recognition of these defects is vital but every bit as important, since it will be fatal if not understood and acted upon, is understanding of the effect of the machine on nature. Until and unless the machine and all the other manifestations of science and technology are interrelated with nature, until their manifold effects are adjusted, human beings will have reason to damn the machine as a master, will continue to be plagued by insecurities. Man will fear and he will run from his fears, carrying with him the neuroses which now characterize so many in the industrialized parts of the world.

Only a big over-all program will come down to the individual, both urban and rural, affecting him intimately. The piecemeal method is doomed to failure. To attempt to solve transportation or housing or education without regard each for the other and for every other of the problems—and for the natural environment as well—always fails. To reshape the whole in full knowledge of the needs of the individual, his interrelationships, and his requirements for adjustment with facilities for living, working, and recreation—and with nature itself—will get results.

Understanding and remedy involves the concentrated attention of specialists in every one of the mental and neurological fields; architects and workers in all the arts; transportation and traffic experts; practitioners of public health and industrial hygiene; educators, recreation experts, as well as social scientists. A full list of those involved would be long indeed, including, as it must, anthropologists, necessary where diverse national origins are the rule, and all types of engineers and other specialists such as were necessary in the building of TVA.

Science is the basis for hope of this and almost every

other forward step even as it is the scourge which makes possible total destruction. Scientists, of all individuals, therefore shoulder a great responsibility, above that carried by others. Most scientists are still content that science remain the handmaiden of private and class interests. The scientist rarely protests though he is given no voice as to how his findings will be used and very little option as to the research he will do. On every side science is used to carry out policies in which it has no say.

In this are the ingredients of new tragedies for the world. In refusing to assume the great social responsibility which is the consequence of their actions, scientists are permitting intelligence to be used for ends which have not been determined intelligently. The world requires the opposite, that science be used in determining policies. When scientists, by word and concerted action, divorce themselves from serving narrow interests, the chances of using freed intelligence for determining and achieving common ends will be infinitely greater.

Some scientists, among them Albert Einstein and Bart J. Bok of Harvard College Observatory, are acutely conscious of this necessity for developing, in Einstein's words, "a sense of responsibility and courage to resist the dangerous inducement to accept work associated with mass destruction." Bok has proposed a revision of the UN Universal Declaration of Human Rights in which would be defined the duty of every scientist:

to examine searchingly the meaning and purposes of the work that he or she is performing, and when in the employ of others, to inquire into these purposes and to evaluate the moral issues that may be involved; to promote the development of science in the ways most beneficial to all mankind and to exert his or her influence as far as possible to prevent its misuse.

It is time for the world to have the benefits of scientists as citizens as well as technicians.

CHAPTER XVIII

Creative Tomorrows

Placed on this isthmus of a middle state,
A being darkly wise, and rudely great: . . .
Created half to rise and half to fall;
Great lord of all things, yet a prey to all;
Sole judge of truth, in endless error hurled;
The glory, jest and riddle of the world.
ALEXANDER POPE

RESEARCH in science produces knowledge which, though tragically misused a large part of the time, is on the whole of tremendous value to the welfare of mankind. But knowledge is much wider than science. In the enormous tides of human behavior, knowledge of matter-of-fact specific occurrences—where they happen and as they happen—becomes increasingly important as scientific knowledge and its application grows.

Population, communication, and cooperation are basic problems in human behavior, evidenced here and now, then and there. Sections of the world are overpopulated. Most of the people on earth are prey to various kinds of discord because communication is unsuccessful and men therefore fail to understand each other.

The failure of communication is part of the greater failure—inability to cooperate and to devise methods of social organization by which cooperation can be effected. All three are paramount human problems in our time and all demand increasing amounts of concentration and attention, if our rapidly accumulating volume of scientific knowledge is to produce better human beings as well as better relationships with the rest of our environment.

In this field of human behavior the need is for accelerated specialized research supported by institutions, by nations, and by the United Nations. The problem of application is literally at the grass roots. The example of Mexico in its "each one-teach one" program of teaching its illiterates blazes this trail. Millions of new teachers, tens of millions of new pupils, accomplishing the first goal—to read and write—can go on to teach and learn the arts of living with profound effects on population, communication, and cooperation.

The entire world shows signs of developing wisdom with which to use all knowledge for common advantage. We have already demonstrated that in the world of science we can speed up the tempo of the evolutionary process as it affects nature. In the field of human behavior the developing international concern for higher standards of living for all peoples and the new techniques where, starting at the very bottom, those who can read and write teach those who cannot, show the evolution of new attitudes affecting behavior. Vistas open which show the end of age-long drifting and the beginning of great realizations, heightening democratic processes while breaking down barriers to human understanding. The oneness of Man and nature can become the basis of a social organization which builds reverence for each man's potential creativeness.

All this can be done. But it takes vision, hope, and courage. Achievement cannot come of itself. Boldness is required. For success depends on revolutionizing our thinking, revolutionizing our action, and having the courage to revolutionize relations among the nations of the world. New attitudes of Man toward Man become imperative as, on the one hand, the creative opportunities become irresistible, and as on the other, the menace of accelerated destructive power becomes unbearable.

In 1944, the most deadly explosive known was cyclamite. Its killing power was 21 deaths per ton. In 1945 came the atomic bomb and the number of deaths per ton moved up to 8000. Present atomic bombs are already admitted to be six times more powerful than was the Hiroshima bomb, which killed 68,000 people and wounded 9000 more. Today's bombs can destroy an area 232 per cent larger than Hiroshima and the hydrogen bomb, on the horizon, would be 1000 times as powerful as the scourge of Hiroshima. Unlocking the atom unleashed a dark titanic force for destruction.

The weight of the menace has crumbled old methods and patterns of control. President Truman's statement that the atom is too big to "be handled on a business-as-usual basis" was a pallid recognition of the revolutionary necessities. Most Americans, along with a large part of the world, sensed the larger truth. Individuals, corporations, or single nations are utterly incapable of dealing with the control and the exploitation of atomic energy. It is a problem which can be solved universally or not at all.

Though universal action, and relief from the overshadowing menace, is not in sight, cherished prejudices in favor of private enterprise have been pushed aside. To insure our survival, we drastically revised long-held conceptions that government had no right to enter production and commerce. Atomic energy became the monopoly of government. In enacting the legislation a majority of Congress, no less than the people who supported the action, responded to the dynamics of the menace. The dynamics had forced change in our institutions and because the change was logical, most people went along with it. The usual group fought it. The anonymous men behind the great corporations, especially the munitions-makers, wanted control of the atom. The military—ever seeking to supplant democratic process with their own authoritarianism —sought it as their private monopoly. Those politicians who serve both these vested interests supported them. When they did not get the atom as their private property, these true apostles of yesterday reverted to the old familiar pattern, whittling away at the original decision. By now, only a few years later, they have encroached more and more on the preserves safeguarded to the people, invading ancient liberties of speech, press, assembly, and of thought. The measure of their success will be the measure of the failure of every man.

The apostles of yesterday may, if we further relax our

vigilance, win their kind of a victory, to the tragic loss of humanity. They cannot stop the mounting pressure. Over the entire world, people seek to find political and social methods of organization which would permanently change the advent of atomic fission from menace to hope. The exigencies, and not theories, have moved the idea of world government from the area of utopian dreaming to the arena of practical discussion. If individual nations cannot by themselves or in agreement with each other control this great force, then the next step, world government, will be taken because it must be. Atomic and hydrogen bomb destruction is too great to live with. No matter who wins, all lose.

If programming, if freeing Man's latent energies, is not done, then Man may lose the prize of the centuries to come. But if all men understand what has been accomplished and what we can go on to achieve with the tools at hand, then it is almost inconceivable that, at the first sign of his approach to maturity, Man will go off on a final wild, atomic bomb fling. To do that he must forget the past, degrade the present, and ignore the future.

When Hitler threatened the world we awoke to find ourselves staring down over the precipice. Then we recognized that we must achieve or die. We achieved—and at a rate that was breathlessly fast because it had to be. Now we look into the abyss of atomic death and we must recognize our danger and, having recognized it, move on to remove the source of our fears.

The fears and the outmoded thinking which would keep us chained to atomic bomb building—to works of destruction—come up now against the courage of the men who will make the future, the men who see in the fullest peaceful release of the energies of the atom the creation of untold resources and the freeing of Man from his heaviest tasks. In that conflict we are being reshaped. In the victory of modern ideas over old-fashioned we will find personal and intimate fulfilment of goals and aspirations.

For many centuries two questions have been in the forefront. What is matter? What is life? The atom has brought to the forefront a third, which has been pressing for attention since Man as a geologic force began to emerge and individuals started to work on projects designed more in the common good than in their own: What is best for Mankind? That question is the abiding brooding query behind the search for a way to eliminate the atomic menace, as it has been the questing exploration of those who have built TVA or have helped, by their thinking and their work, to alleviate disease. It is the key question, and it is possible to ask it and to answer it because Man has progressed so far along the road that the unity of all mankind is now widely recognized. The will, the imagination, and the evidence exist to prove to each single individual that all of us together possess power and strength greater than that of the atomic bomb. The value of the individual can only be enhanced if the value of all men is increased.

Herman Melville once said, "Men may seem detestable as joint stock companies and nations; knaves, fools and murderers they may be; men may have mean and meagre faces; but Man, in the ideal, is so noble and so sparkling, such a grand and glowing creature, that over any ignominious blemish in him all his fellows should run to throw their costliest robes."

As we stop the old-fashioned damage in every field, whether urban or rural, industrial or agricultural, we will see more rather than less of "Man, in the ideal" and we will find more of the answers to the great overriding question, "What is best for Mankind?" The mounting struggle for justice, which marks the emergence of colonial peoples and national minorities, is part of the answer. The almost universal recognition of the necessity for a fair distribution of nature's bounty is another facet, implicit in nurturing, conserving, and expanding all resources. All the parts of the great answer come from Man's increasing ability to use his mind, coupled with a determination to use that ability for constructive ends. Everyone is now able to participate in the quest and to take pleasure from doing it. In America almost every child is able to discourse learnedly on the complicated mechanics of radio, automobiles, and even the atomic bomb—demonstrating that complexity need not be a deterrent to enjoyment for huge numbers of people. The problem is to give that capacity to understand some point, to make it part of the around-the-clock pattern of living, as has been already done by so many, and especially by those scientists who have shown the world that their complicated and extremely difficult activities give them an engrossing enjoyment far beyond that which most people get from hobbies and sports.

The truth is that the men and women now involved in reshaping the planet are having all the best of it. Already they have found out what so many more will learn. It is more fun to repair the planet and the societies of men who live on it than it is to repair an automobile or a radio.

In the United States the outstanding scientists and engineers have teamed with the most unselfish and far-sighted politicians to develop shelter belts, to promote soil conservation, to control disease, to create—in hundreds of other ways—better living conditions for all. No individual, no giant corporations reap profits from TVA; yet the Roosevelts, the Pinchots, the Norrises, the Lilienthals, and the other TVA planners and administrators have taken a satisfaction from the achievement which is greater by far than that which the executives of the biggest corporation could get from record earnings.

The individual identified with TVA earned a dividend. His return was, on a social scale, the same as that felt by an artist who has produced a masterpiece. Both feel the greatest of all satisfactions—that feeling of the creator of works which all men enjoy. This creative field, great works for the benefit of all men, is a new area of social activity and TVA marked its true inception in this country.

The people of the world have mind and imagination big

enough to see their world whole. They can project their minds anywhere and they can accomplish with zest that which they plan. This is the talent which makes of the future a dramatic and exciting adventure. This is the time as never before to dream the big dreams, to plan the big projects, to work on the big teams which are gaited and geared for the doing of that which is most important. The challenge and the opportunity are ever so much bigger than any which men have ever faced before.

The dream can be realized. It began with the little-noticed but steadily progressive development of the mind and the nervous system, and it has taken us now within sight of the realization of that ideal of Man which Melville saw. We must get on toward that realization. The way will be rough.

The transition from one epoch into another is bound to be stormy, and this, being Man's greatest transition, is already proving the most turbulent of all historical periods. The old-fashioned minds—tied as they are to custom, habits, and prejudices which are losing their validity—make a desperate effort to hold back the new, to keep the old. Out of their resistance on all fronts has come the successive acts of great tragedy through which we live. If we are to succeed we must understand their motivation and behavior and see behind their words. Only then can we do the things necessary to achieve the best use of the new strength which we have acquired as a geological force, strength which makes it possible to provide a floor for creative living for all. The world can be reshaped—"for humanity possesses the knowledge and the skill." The old-fashioned men hold us back.

The times are overripe for action by America. In the midst of the Civil War, Emerson called for "an affirmative step in the interests of human civility." "It is very certain," he wrote, "that the statesman who shall break through the cobwebs of doubt, fear and petty cavil that lie in the way will be greeted by the unanimous thanks of Mankind."

America with its might, its wealth, and its democratic traditions has the power now to take that "affirmative step," rendering a world racked by doubt and insecurity a supreme service.

The issue still hangs in the balance. It will remain undecided until the knowledge is universal that Man has elementally chosen the right path into this latest in the many stages of geologic history; the first to be in tune with democratic ideals.

Man is now a planetary force and his impact on the earth will be greater than that of an Ice Age. The ice moved without direction, scouring rocks into soil, leaving lake beds and valleys behind it. Man changes the earth in just those ways and many others. Man, because he has the benefit of mind and direction, changes his environment where he finds it desirable to effect the change. The results will be epochal, comparable to that stage at the dawn of history which ushered in the green forests where Man made his first appearance. The vision is fascinating. In it is a promise which invites hope and confidence for a glorious future in which Man's progress will be like that of one of his own inventions—the airplane. That machine, which cannot go backwards and is so unsteady as to need propping when stationary, once in motion achieves dynamic stability —dependent on its forward movement. As Man's brain cannot retrogress, so the dynamic stability of the new age will save mankind from the recurring dives into famine and barbarian war which have marked its trek up to now.

As we achieve dynamic stability we will enjoy the fruits of physical well-being; but this cannot be an end. The new era can give the world taller, stronger, and richer men everywhere, but it must also produce better human beings qualitatively.

For too long the individual has had, as Thoreau said, to be almost exclusively occupied and profoundly disturbed by his uncertain chances of obtaining necessary food, shelter, clothing, and fuel. His need for these has driven him into corners of frustration, into herds propelled by demagogues and dictators who promise solutions and cannot deliver them. The next half century can finally dispose of these problems and prepare each person to meet the deeper and truer problems in an atmosphere of freedom. The maturing of the individual in full recognition of his relationship with all mankind is the grand design.

Men can remake themselves and their culture. An improved race of Man and a culture so rich that we cannot even conjecture its varied texture await us ahead. Treasures beyond dreams of the most avaricious are just over the horizon. All the world is in our grasp, yet we stand on the brink in trembling and in fear. Will the blind and the power-hungry old-fashioned despoilers combine with the ignorant to push the world over the abyss? It will not be so. The future is in our hands. We will not let it go.

INDEX

Africa, 163-64
Age of the Mind, 183
Agricultural revolution, 160-61
Alabama, 37
Albuquerque, 85-86
Aleman, President, 139
American Public Power Association, 21
Anaconda Copper Company, 74, 81, 88, 89
Anti-trust laws, 51
Arizona, 87, 126
Asia, 48
Atomic bomb, 194, 196, 197
Atomic energy, 142, 170, 195, 197
and industry, 170
Atomic Energy Commission, 105
Atomic fission, 3, 169
Australia, 138
Ayres, Eugene, 164

Baltimore, 131
Biosphere, 177, 182
Birth control, 7, 12, 155-57, 161
Black Sea, 181
Bok, Bart J., 190
Bonneville, 23
Boyd-Orr, Lord, 147
World Food Board, 147-49
Brannan, 148
Brazil, 20, 135, 152
Brentano, L., 11
Bromfield, Louis, 131
Buffon, 177
Burbank, Luther, 182

California, 21, 24, 25, 37, 39, 86
water problem, 128-130, 180

Canada, 152
Catholic Church, 156, 157
Ceylon, 105
Clark, Colin, 11
Claude, Georges, 168
Cobbett, 8
Colorado, 87, 109
Colorado-Big Thompson Trans-Mountain Diversion Project, 180
Colorado River, 83, 86
Columbia River, 26, 83, 86, 180
Columbia Valley Authority, 22
Communication, 192-93
Congress, 24, 25, 39, 110, 111, 116, 131
Cooke, Morris L., 136
Cooperation, 192-93
Crowther, J. G., 142

Damoder Valley Corporation, 136-138
Dana, J. D., 177
Darwin, 177
Day and Zimmerman Project, 152
Dead Sea, 141
Denmark, farming in, 158
standard of living of, 158
Des Moines River, 93
Dewey, Thomas E., 112
Dixiecrats, 37-39
Drought, 64, 77-79, 92, 98
DuPont Company, 51, 171, 172
Dust Bowl, 77-79

Edison Electric Institute, 22
Education, 154, 193
Einstein, Albert, 190

Electric Bond & Share Company, 81
Electric Power, 26, 30, 32, 49, 69,
    138, 163, 185
    general role of, 26, 27, 30, 115
    and agriculture, 27
    and farming, 29
    and industry, 27-29, 31, 49
    and labor, 27, 28
    and resources, 27
    and soil, 31
Electrical Industry, *see* Utility com-
    panies
Elephant Butte Reservoir, 86
Energy, sources,
    earth heat, 168
    solar, 164-169
    tides, 168, 169
England, *see* Great Britain
Europe, 42, 48

Fall, Albert B., 38
Farmers' Union, 119
Farming, 56, 88, 108, 118, 119,
    128-130, 150, 151, 153, 154,
    157-160
    and electric power, 27-29
    as industry, 160
Federal Power Commission, 21, 73
Federal Trade Commission, 53
Fertilizer, 31, 47, 49, 53, 73, 74, 88
Floods, 60-66, 76, 77, 85, 92-95,
    103-105
    control of, 27, 47, 58, 61, 64, 65,
    67, 69, 85, 92, 94, 96, 104, 105
Florida, 37
Food, 6, 8, 25, 147
    production, 148-150, 159
    reserve, 147, 148
    sources, 151, 152
    supply, 7, 153
    surplus, 148, 149
    wastage, 151
Forestry, 59, 69
Forestry Service, 76
Forests, 76, 82, 119

French West Africa, 137
Fuel, role of, 162, 163
    shortage of, 162

General Electric Company, 82
General Motors, 51
Geneva Steel Plant, 89, 90
Georgia, 37
Germany, 144
Geyser, California, 168
Great Britain, 6, 138, 146
    farming, 158
    utility system, 33
Great Central Valley, 52, 128-131,
    153, 180
Great Central Valley Project, 21, 25
Gulf Oil Company, 35

Heat pump, 168
Hitler, 3, 114, 196
Hiroshima, 194
Hopson, 22
Hoover Commission, 75
Hoover, Herbert, 68
Hudson River, 66

Idaho, 86, 88, 109
India, 102, 136-137, 139, 144
Industry, 18, 26-27, 31, 45, 48, 51-
    52, 88, 108
    as resource, 174
Institute of International Education,
    152
Insull, Samuel, 22
Iran, 152
Israel, 20, 100, 139, 140-142

Japan, 157
Jordan River Valley, 20, 105, 139

Kansas City, 80
Kellogg, Charles E., 14
Kings River Project, 21
Korea, 152

Labor, 119-120
Langmuir, Dr. Irving, 182

Le Conte, Joseph, 177
Lee, Robert E., 67-68
Liberia, 152
Lilienthal, David E., 105-06
Loch Sloy Dam, 138
Locke, Colonel Jerome, 75
Los Angeles, 86, 127
Louisiana, 37
Lowdermilk, Walter C., 139-40

Maine, utility companies, 33
Malthus, 6-9
  Essay on Population, 6
  Malthusianism, 116
  Malthusian Law, 6
  "natural law," 8
  neo-Malthusian, 9, 18-19
Man, 1-2, 6
  creates resources, 18
  and evolution, 176-77
  future of, 194, 196-201
  increasing knowledge of, 178
  and industry, 45, 48
  and machine, 188-89
  and nature, 9, 13-14, 19, 97-99,
    101-02, 104, 177-181, 188, 201
  as a resource, 12-13
  and science, 4, 12, 189, 192
  technical advance, 179, 181, 183
Massachusetts Institute of Technol-
  ogy, 165
McCabe, Dr. Louis, 133
Mediterranean Sea, 141
Mexico, 102, 139, 154, 193
  Ministry of Hydroelectric Re-
    sources, 139
  Papaloapan River Project, 139
Middle East, 41-43, 142
Minifie, James M., 44
Mississippi, 37, 81
Mississippi River, 64, 66, 69, 93,
  132-33
Missouri, 95
Missouri River, 30, 61, 64-67, 70-74,
  79-80, 83, 88, 91-95, 109

Missouri Valley, 19, 22-23, 26, 48,
  58, 60, 77-78, 80, 91, 96, 103,
  106-08, 110-11, 139, 163
  future of, 110-12, 115-16
Missouri Valley Authority, 20, 27,
  48, 52, 70, 72, 112, 115-16,
  121, 132
Montana, 73, 80-81, 87-88, 109
Montana Power Company, 73, 88
Musser, R. H., 95
Mussolini, 114

National Association of Electric
  Companies, 20
National Rural Electric Cooperative
  Association, 21
Nature, and man, 9, 13-14, 19, 97-
  102, 104, 177-181, 188, 201
Natural resources, 6, 26, 33, 46, 52,
  100, 143
  abuse of, 52-54, 56-58, 80-82,
    107
  conservation of, 26-27, 119-20,
    187
  exploitation of, 27, 109, 141-42
  neglect of, 106-09
  role in modern world, 5
  substitution, 172-74
Navigation, 27, 58, 61, 65, 67, 69,
  101, 185
Negeb Desert, 100, 141-42, 153
Nehru, Pandit, 136-38
New Deal, 112
New England, pollution in, 123
New Mexico, 85
New York, 123
New York City, 131, 181
New York Harbor, 66
Niger River Dam, 137
Norris, Senator George, 16, 72
North Dakota, 109

Oceans, man's influence on, 180
Office of Air and Stream Pollution
  Prevention Research, 133

Ohio, 131
Ohio River, 66
Ohio Valley, 66
Oil, 34, 48, 163, 171
  and power, 40
  reserves, 38, 41, 44
  shortage, 40, 42-43
Oil industry, 35-41, 43, 47
  political power, 41-42, 47
Olds, Leland, 21
O'Mahoney, Senator Joseph, 130

Pacific Gas & Electric Company, 21-24
Palestine, see Israel
Palomar, 181
Pearl, Raymond, 11
Pennsylvania, utility companies, 33
  water, 123, 126
Philadelphia, water pollution, 123
Pick, General Lewis A., 65, 70, 94
Pick Plan, 70-72
Pick-Sloan Plan, 72-78, 94, 103
Pittsburgh, 89
Population, 6-11, 17, 25-26, 45, 107,
  155, 157, 192-97
Proctor & Gamble, 131

Queensland, 152

Railroads, 30, 70, 88, 90
Reclamation Law, 129
Regional planning, 103
Rio Grande River, 36, 83, 85-86
Rockefeller Basic Economy Corporation, 152
Rocky Mountains, 81-87, 91, 180
Roosevelt, F. D., 112
Roosevelt, Theodore, 129
Roper, Elmo, 113
Rural Electrical Associations, 23, 118
Russell, Bertrand, 170
Russia, see Soviet Union

Sahara Desert, 142, 153
Sacramento River, 179-180

St. Lawrence River, 26, 32
St. Louis, 80, 92-93
San Francisco, 181
San Francisco River, 20, 135
San Francisco Valley Authority, 135
San Juaquin River, 179-80
Scandinavia, 3
Science, 4, 20, 192
  and agriculture, 149-50, 152, 154-55, 160
  effect on human life, 5
  as resource, 18, 174
  as social responsibility, 190-91
  standard of living, 19
Senate Committee on Small Business, 40, 43
Shasta Dam, 24, 130
Shell Oil Corporation, 35
Sloan Plan, see Pick-Sloan
Smog, 133-34
Soil, conservation, 69, 119-20, 199
  deterioration, 14-15, 83, 87
  erosion, 82-87, 92, 95, 98, 103, 120, 133
  exploitation, 150
  irrigation, 27, 58, 69, 75, 91, 127, 179
  reclamation, 153, 181
  as resource, 31
Solar radiation, 165-67
Soviet Union, 3, 42, 142, 144, 146, 152, 158, 181
Standard of living, 10, 12, 16, 19, 24, 45, 49-50, 107, 152, 161-162, 170
Standard Oil Company, 35-36, 42-43
State Public Service Commissions, 22
Steel Industry, 46-48, 89-90
Stettinius Plan, 152
Straus, Michael, 87
Sun Oil Company, 35

Tennessee River, 185
Tennessee Valley, 15, 19, 97, 112, 115

Tennessee Valley Authority, 3, 19,
23-24, 105-06, 110, 113, 115,
117, 143-44, 184-85, 197, 199
as a cultural value, 186
and democracy, 186-87
and electric power, 17
and farming, 16-17
and forestry, 17
history of, 15-16, 20, 24-25
influence of, 16, 105-06, 136-42
and population, 17
significance, 110-13, 135-36
as social organization, 97, 102,
185-86
and standard of living, 16-17
steam plants, 24-25
success of, 199
and utility companies, 20-27
Teton Range, 87
Texas, 34-37, 87, 126
Tidelands, 38-39, 43, 47
decision on, 37
Trade associations, 22
Truman, Harry S., 21, 45-46, 112,
194
"Bold New Program," 145-148

Union Pacific Railroad Company, 81
United Nations, 145, 147, 151, 193
Food and Agriculture Organiza-
tion, 152, 154-55
Universal Declaration of Human
Rights, 190
World Economic Report, July,
1949, 50
U.S. Army Engineers, 26, 60-79, 87,
92-94
U. S. Bureau of Land Management,
87
U. S. Bureau of Mines, 87, 133
U. S. Bureau of Reclamation, 69-72,
87, 130
U. S. Chamber of Commerce, 26

U. S. Department of Agriculture,
14, 76
U. S. Department of Interior, 38,
131
U. S. Fish and Wildlife Service, 87
U. S. Geologic Survey, 127
U. S. Indian Service, 87
U. S. Public Health Service, 123
U. S. Soil Conservation Service, 95
U. S. Supreme Court, 37-38, 59
on natural resources, 59
U. S. Treasury, 77
United States Rubber Company, 51
United States Steel Corporation, 89-
90
Utah, 86, 89-90
Utility companies, 20-23, 25-26, 33,
47, 70, 73
lobby, 22, 24, 33
vs. T.V.A., 20-27

Vernadsky, V. I., 176
Vesuvius, 168
Vogt, William, 9

Water, 98, 101, 122-23, 132, 185
exploitation, 179-80
industrial needs, 126
pollution, 123-25, 127, 131-32
pollution control, 27, 123, 125-26
reservoirs, 27, 71, 76, 132
shortage, 109, 122, 126, 128,
131-32
supply, 27, 125-27, 142, 182
waste of, 129
Water power, waste of, 73-75
Watershed, 82-83, 86-88, 90, 100-01,
132
Weizmann, Chaim, 142
Westinghouse, 82
Wyoming, 80, 86-87, 109

Youngstown Sheet & Tube Company, 131